THE EPISTLE OF JAMES

AND OTHER DISCOURSES

THE EPISTLE OF JAMES

AND OTHER DISCOURSES

BY R. W. DALE, LL.D

BIRMINGHAM

Wipf and Stock Publishers
199 W 8th Ave, Suite 3
Eugene, OR 97401

The Epistle of James and Other Discourses
By Dale, R. W.
ISBN: 1-59752-644-4
Publication date 4/14/2006
Previously published by Hodder and Stoughton, 1895

EDITOR'S PREFACE

MOST of the Sermons contained in the second part of this volume had been revised by my father, and several have already appeared in the *British Weekly*, or elsewhere; in preparing them for publication, therefore, only some slight alterations were required. In the first part, however, this was not the case. Some of the discourses were not consecutive, and these had to be rearranged or recast. Here and there a few sentences have been added or local allusions omitted. But wherever it was possible, the original form has been scrupulously retained.

My father, I know, would have wished special reference to be made to the Rev. J. B. Mayor's *Commentary on the Epistle of James*, which he read with interest and delight during the summer of last year, shortly before these discourses were preached;

he borrowed from it freely—and as freely acknowledged his indebtedness. For myself, I have to thank Mr. E. A. Lawrence of Halifax for much help and many valuable suggestions in the task of revision.

A. W. W. DALE.

TRINITY HALL, CAMBRIDGE,
October 16, 1895.

CONTENTS

PART I

PART II

PART I

I

JAMES, THE BROTHER OF OUR LORD

'James, a servant of God and of the Lord Jesus Christ, to the twelve tribes which are of the Dispersion, greeting.'—JAMES i. 1.

IT seems to me practically certain that James, the writer of this epistle, was not one of the twelve apostles. He is mentioned by Paul in the Epistle to the Galatians,[1] and is there described as our Lord's brother, and he is mentioned several times in the Acts of the Apostles. He was the chief minister—the Bishop—of the Christian Church in Jerusalem, a church which naturally consisted of Jewish believers in our Lord, and he was the head of that great party in the Church, which continued to observe the customs of Judaism long after our Lord had been crucified and had risen from the dead. Those Jewish teachers, therefore, who insisted that Paul's converts among the heathen were under an obligation to keep the Jewish law, naturally appealed to the example and authority of James.

We can easily imagine their line of argument. They would tell the heathen men in Galatia and elsewhere, who had become Christians through Paul's

[1] Gal. i. 19.

preaching, that the Church in Jerusalem, which consisted largely of men and women who had known the Lord Jesus Christ, were still Jews in their manner of life, and that their chief minister, our Lord's own brother, was rigid in his observance of Jewish practices. The controversy became acute. Paul said that converts from heathenism need not observe Jewish customs; these Jewish teachers said,—James observes them; the members of the Church at Jerusalem observe them; our Lord Himself observed them, and never abolished them. There was an appeal to James, and to the Apostles living in Jerusalem, and to the whole Church in that city.[1] The decision reached was this: that though Jewish Christians might retain their natural habits and continue to observe the customs of their fathers, Gentile Christians were under no obligation to keep the Jewish law; but they were charged to 'abstain from things sacrificed to idols and from blood, and from things strangled, and from fornication.' Sensual vice was so common among the heathen that the Christian Gentiles are specially warned against it; and other things were forbidden, in order that the Gentile Christians might not wound and distress their Jewish brethren, and that it might be possible for Christian Jews and Christian Gentiles to have friendly social relations with each other.

James was the leader of the Jewish party in the Church, but he recognised the divine mission of

[1] Acts xv. 24-29.

Paul, and exerted his immense influence to prevent the Judaising teachers from hindering Paul's work and breaking up the Churches which Paul had founded among the heathen.

James, in my judgment, I repeat, was not one of the twelve Apostles. He must not, therefore, be confounded with the Apostle James, whom Herod beheaded about fourteen years after the crucifixion of our Lord. Nor must he be confounded with another of the Apostles, who was called James the Little, the son of Cleopas.

He does not call himself an apostle in this epistle. He describes himself as '*a servant*'—or bond-servant, or slave—'*of God and of the Lord Jesus Christ*'; nor does the writer of the Epistle of Jude call himself an apostle. He describes himself as 'a slave (or bond-servant) of Jesus Christ, and brother of James.'[1] Every one would know that by James was meant the famous Bishop of the Church in Jerusalem, who, both on account of the strength of his own character and his relationship to our Lord, held so great a place among the Jewish Christians. The names of both brothers occur together in the Gospel of Matthew. When our Lord taught in the synagogue at Nazareth, the people asked, 'whence hath this man this wisdom, and these mighty works? Is not this the carpenter's son? is not his mother called Mary, and his brethren, James, and Joseph, and Simon, and Judas?'[2] Judas is the same as Jude.

[1] Jude i. 1.

[2] Matt. xiii. 54, 55.

John tells us that even the brethren of our Lord did not believe on Him.[1] If two of His brethren had been apostles,—if even one had been an apostle, it would have been impossible for John to say this. If later in our Lord's ministry two of His brethren had believed in Him, one of them becoming afterwards so great a person as James, the Bishop of Jerusalem, we should surely have had some notice of it. John would hardly have left all our Lord's brothers under the reproach of unbelief, if during our Lord's earthly life any one of them had acknowledged that He was the Christ.

The question has been raised whether these brothers of our Lord—James, and Joseph, and Simon, and Judas, and His sisters—were the children of Joseph and Mary, or whether they were the children of Joseph by a previous marriage, so that they were not really His brothers and sisters, but only Joseph's children with whom He was brought up. The question will be determined by individual feeling; there is no strong evidence to incline the judgment either one way or the other. It is said, indeed, that if Joseph, and James, and Simon, and Judas had been the children of our Lord's own mother, our Lord when on the Cross would not have commended her to the care of the Apostle John. But there is no real force in this objection. In the first place, John was the son of Salome, and Salome was almost certainly the sister of Mary,

[1] John vii. 5.

our Lord's mother, so that John would be her nephew; and if her own sons did not believe in the Lord Jesus, that would create a wide separation between them and Mary, and at such a time she could hardly be happy in their home. She would receive more sympathy in her sorrow from her nephew John, who was the beloved disciple of our Lord.

At present, then, we have these three points clear: (1) the writer of this epistle was a brother of our Lord; that is, he was either the son of Joseph by a former marriage or the son of Joseph and Mary, and in either case he was brought up with the Lord Jesus Christ. (2) He was not one of the original apostles. (3) During Christ's earthly life he did not believe that Jesus, his brother, was the Christ.

But our Lord appears to James after His resurrection. Paul tells us this in his account of the appearances of the risen Christ.[1] Some have thought that it was by this appearance to him that James came to believe. We cannot tell; but if so, this would be contrary to the general law which seems to have controlled our Lord's appearances. He appeared to those who were already His disciples, to confirm their faith; not to unbelievers, to create faith. I prefer to think that when James heard from Mary, his mother, and from the apostles that Jesus had risen from the dead, his unbelief gave way. He must have been filled with remorse for not having believed before,

[1] 1 Cor. xv. 7.

and Christ appeared to him to strengthen his faith and to give him consolation.

He became a member of the Church in Jerusalem, and after a few years he became the Bishop of that Church ; which means nothing more than that he was its principal minister; and he was the head of the Jewish party in the Church.

The traditions about him, which are recorded by a writer in the next century, are in many respects untrustworthy, but beneath them there is no doubt a ground of solid fact. He is represented as a man of extraordinary righteousness, in the old Jewish sense; walking in all the commandments of the Lord blameless, observing with great exactness all Jewish customs in relation to fasting, and prayer, and food, and all other matters. The traditions also say that he was a Rechabite ; that is, he was brought up like John the Baptist, so that from his birth he never drank wine or strong drink, never had his hair cut, and never took a bath. If these traditions are true, they suggest that the children in that home of Nazareth were brought up under an austere and rigid discipline. And this makes it the more remarkable that our Lord Himself, when He reached manhood, gave up the severity of His earlier habits, so that men contrasted His way of life with the way of John the Baptist. And perhaps this may also throw light on the unbelief of James and the rest of His brothers. When Christ began to live a life so much freer than theirs, when He broke through the austere restraint which they had associated with the highest forms of righteousness, they would find it difficult to believe that He was really a religious teacher sent from God. But James came to believe at last, and was a great personage among those who confessed that Jesus was the Christ. He too discovered how great our Lord was. He does not presume to describe himself as the brother of our Lord, though other men so described him. He is *the servant, the slave, of God and of our Lord Jesus Christ.*

His Epistle has an interest of its own. He retained so much of his Judaism, even after he became a Christian, that his Epistle in its spirit and colour has almost as much of the Old Testament in it as of the New. He speaks like a Jewish prophet as well as like a preacher of Christ.

And the Jews to whom the Epistle was addressed also retained a good deal of their Judaism. They called their Christian assembly the Synagogue, and the sins against which they were warned are the sins to which Christian Jews were specially liable. It seems probable that while the Epistle was meant for Jews everywhere, James, when he wrote it, was thinking most of the great Jewish populations that occupied a considerable part of the country between the Euphrates and the Tigris. About the time that he was writing, great calamities were descending upon them. They had become rich and prosperous, but the fierce storm which a few years later broke upon Jerusalem with such awful severity,—which destroyed the city and the Temple, and finally scattered the nation,—broke first upon the Jews of Babylonia. These calamities were what we still call 'trials,'—trials of the strength and constancy of faith. They brought desolation to innumerable homes. The sufferings were of many kinds; they tested courage and endurance and loyalty in many ways, and though James was addressing Jews in all parts of the world, there is but little doubt that he was thinking mainly of those who were then passing through this cruel and severe affliction.

II

THE GOSPEL OF SUFFERING

'*Count it all joy, my brethren, when ye fall into manifold temptations; knowing that the proof of your faith worketh patience. And let patience have its perfect work, that ye may be perfect and entire, lacking in nothing.*

'*But if any of you lacketh wisdom, let him ask of God, who giveth to all liberally and upbraideth not; and it shall be given him. But let him ask in faith, nothing doubting: for he that doubteth is like the surge of the sea driven by the wind and tossed. For let not that man think that he shall receive anything of the Lord; a double-minded man, unstable in all his ways.*

'*But let the brother of low degree glory in his high estate: and the rich, in that he is made low: because as the flower of the grass he shall pass away. For the sun ariseth with the scorching wind, and withereth the grass; and the flower thereof falleth, and the grace of the fashion of it perisheth: so also shall the rich man fade away in his goings.*'—JAMES i. 2-11.

THE Epistle opens in an heroic strain. '*Count it all joy,*' James says, '*when ye fall into manifold temptations, knowing that the proof of your faith*—that which tests its strength—*worketh patience.*' This is a stern doctrine. These trials bring misery, he says, but you Christian men and women are to look beyond them, and to find the light even in the misery. Why? Because the trials discipline you to patience; and he adds, '*Let patience have its perfect work.*' Do not give way after you have borne suffering well for a time, else all will be lost. Be faithful, as our Lord says to the Church at Smyrna,—'be faithful unto death.' Endure not merely bitter persecution, loss of property, loss of liberty, but carry your faithfulness through to the last extremity. 'Be faithful unto death, and I will give thee the crown of life.' Or, as James puts it, '*Let patience have its perfect work, that ye may be perfect and entire, lacking in nothing.*'

This, I say, is stern doctrine. To count it all joy when suffering comes upon us, and suffering that tests our faith, how is this possible? It is only possible when we come to think of righteousness as being infinitely more precious than comfort, happiness, or peace; when we come to see that the great thing for us in this life is not to enjoy ease and prosperity, to get rich, to rise in the world, but to become better men. For this we require wisdom,—a true estimate of the nature and ends of human life.

'*If any of you lacketh wisdom let him ask of God.*' *Wisdom* was a great word among the Jews, especially during the centuries immediately before Christ. There was a distinct class of Jewish literature called The Wisdom literature, represented by the Book of Proverbs, and the Book of Ecclesiastes, and the Book of Job. 'The wise men,' says Professor Driver, 'took for granted the main postulates of Israel's creed, and applied themselves rather to the observation of human character as such, seeking to analyse conduct, studying action in its consequences, and establishing morality, upon the basis of principles common to humanity at large. . . . They have been termed . . . the Humanists of Israel. Their teaching had a practical aim.' It related to conduct and to education. And further, 'the observation of human nature . . . naturally leads on to reflection on the problems which it presents.'[1] The inequalities among men, the prosperity of bad men, the sufferings of good men, the apparent vanity of human pursuits,—these problems are discussed in Job and Ecclesiastes. And so when James speaks of wisdom, he means a true understanding of human life, and of the moral order of the world—the power and habit of forming a just judgment on wealth and poverty, joy and sorrow, ease and pain, public honour and public dishonour, and all the incidents of human experience,—a clear vision of the laws which should regulate conduct, of the principles which should form character. It is, as some one has said, a living insight into Christian duty; it is the art of Christian conduct. '*If any man lack this wisdom let him ask of God.*'

We all greatly need it, for there are large numbers of Christian men and women who not only mean well, but who at times set their hearts very earnestly on doing well; yet they make nothing of it. There is no dignity or force or consistency in their life. You can see the traces and outlines of a noble plan, but the plan has never been carried out. They dis-

[1] Driver, *Introduction to the Literature of the Old Testament*, p. 369.

cover their mistakes too late to mend them—mistakes in their personal habits, mistakes in the ordering of their homes, mistakes in the choice of their friends, mistakes in the objects for which they have spent time and money and strength. 'Experience,' as Coleridge says, 'is too often like the stern-lights of a ship; it illuminates only the path over which we have travelled, and it gives no enlightenment or guidance for conduct in the future.' We want this divine gift of wisdom, the power to judge things according to their true worth, and in their relation to our own plan of life. It shows us what life really is, and how we are to make the best of it.

James implies that if we had it we should count it all joy when we fall into trouble. What a difference that would make to many of us! And even if we came short of rejoicing, and were only able to subdue our discontent and impatience, and to rise above the transient troubles to the eternal treasure which it cannot lessen, the eternal glory which it cannot dim, how great a thing it would be! This wisdom, if we had it, would transfigure life. You have an unreasonable employer; wisdom would teach you to regard his unreasonableness as a divinely appointed discipline to train you to good temper. A man has greatly wronged you; wisdom would teach you to regard the wrong as giving you the opportunity of fulfilling our Lord's precept: 'Bless them that curse you, pray for them that despitefully use you.' Your occupation is dreary, monotonous, badly paid;

wisdom will teach you to do your work as unto the Lord and not unto men, and this will bring down into your work-room light from heaven. You lose money that you have worked hard for; wisdom will teach you that this loss will help you not to put your trust in uncertain riches. And so when a man once comes to see that human life is surrounded by infinite horizons, all things will be changed; conduct will have a new law, the heart will find new peace.

The objects for which a man will spend his time and strength and money will be changed. With regard to many things to which he has attached great importance, he will cease to care for them, and will feel that they do not concern him. When Napoleon was in the East it was suggested to him that he should visit Jerusalem. 'No,' he answered, 'Jerusalem does not come within the field of my operations.' That was the kind of answer that such a man was likely to make; it suggests one of the great secrets of his greatness; he saw what would count for the success of his campaign, and he cared for nothing else. And wisdom will enable us to discern what are the true ends of life, and how we are to secure them. As for what would not contribute to these, we shall say they do not come into the field of our operations; they count for nothing: I will spend no time on them, no thought, no money. There are higher aims and loftier purposes than those—achieving righteousness, winning God's favour, securing eternal glory. These are the objects towards which we press.

These are the supreme motives for those whose eyes wisdom has opened to see things as they are,—to whom wisdom has revealed the inner law of life.

And if we '*lack wisdom*,' we are to '*ask of God, who giveth to all liberally*'—freely, unconditionally, making no bargain—'*and upbraideth not*.' If we discover that we are wanting wisdom, are troubled by the want of it, and ask for it, He will not rebuke us for our folly. But, says James, '*let him ask in faith, nothing doubting; for he that doubteth is like the surge of the sea driven by the wind and tossed. For let not that man think that he shall receive anything of the Lord; a double-minded man, unstable in all his ways*.'

These last words suggest a long train of reflection, which we cannot now pursue. The man who has some confidence in God and yet doubts, who asks for wisdom, hopes that God will give it, and yet is uncertain,—he is '*a double-minded man*.' He will not only be hesitating in his prayers, he will be '*unstable in all his ways*.' That is the trouble with many of us—high thoughts to-day, to-morrow they have all disappeared.

Now look at the words which follow: '*Let the brother of low degree glory in his high estate: and the rich, in that he is made low; because as the flower of the grass he shall pass away. For the sun ariseth with the scorching wind, and withereth the grass; and the flower thereof falleth, and the grace of the fashion of it perisheth : so also shall the rich man fade away in his goings.'*

'*Let the brother of low degree*'—the poor man, the obscure man,—'*glory in his high estate* ;' he is a child of God through Christ, heir of eternal blessedness; instead of resenting his poverty and being discontented with his obscurity, let him remember that he is a prince, and glory in it. He is a prince on his way to his kingdom, travelling by rough roads, enduring many hardships, suffering from hunger, cold, and weariness, and the people among whom he is travelling do not know anything about his greatness; but *he* knows; '*let him glory in his high estate.*'

It is a hard thing for a Christian man to maintain this high and cheerful temper while he is enduring hardships. The hardships are so near, so real, so distressing, that they fill all his thoughts. How is it possible for him not to be depressed? It is only possible when he really comes to see how brief are his earthly sufferings when compared with eternal joy, how light they are when compared with eternal glory. Let him look at things as they are; let him have true wisdom, wisdom to form right judgments about this world and the next, about earthly sorrows and divine blessings, and then the brother of low degree will '*glory in his high estate.*'

On the other hand, the rich brother is to glory '*in that he is made low.*' That is harder still. He is to glory in whatever reminds him that his wealth is transient, that he will cease to be a rich man when he dies, and may cease to be a rich man long before he dies. So far as he is merely a rich man and nothing more, '*as the flower of the grass he shall pass away. For the sun ariseth with the scorching wind, and withereth the grass, and the flower thereof falleth, and the grace of the fashion of it perisheth : so also shall the rich man fade away in his goings.*' The rich man is very likely to forget all this. He is likely to pride himself on his wealth, as though it were an enduring possession, to find his satisfaction in the pleasant things of life, to forget how brief these satisfactions are, and to disregard the awful, the glorious life which lies beyond death. He is likely to think too highly of himself because his wealth purchases him the consideration of others. He is likely to become self-confident, to be masterful and arrogant, to suppose that because he is better off than his Christian brother he is therefore a better man.

Let us translate James's meaning into modern language. If a bank breaks and he loses a large sum of money, the rich man must rejoice, because it compels him to see that he may lose everything, and that he is just as dependent on God as the poorest of his brethren. If he invests half his fortune in a rotten company, and is obliged to live in a smaller house and to part with his horses and carriages, he is to rejoice, because it forces him to think of the treasure which moth doth not corrupt and which thieves cannot steal. That is very hard. If he finds that with all his riches he cannot get into the kind of society which he likes, that poorer men win more affection and more respect,—if in any way he is humbled, he is to rejoice; for it makes him see the difference between what he has and what he is. What he has will soon disappear, and the great question for him to consider is what he is. And he may discover that his money represents all that he is worth, and that apart from his money he is worthless. He is to '*glory in that he is made low*,'—in whatever makes clearer the real truth about himself and his wealth he is to rejoice; it is always best to know how we really stand, though the knowledge may be very painful to us. That a rich man should glory in whatever brings him down from his imagined security of eminence is, I repeat, a hard lesson to learn, and a rich man needs a great deal of the grace of God to learn it.

However, there are very few, if any, of us who are subjected to this severe test. Compared with the rich and the great, we are all, I suppose, '*brothers of low degree*,'—not wealthy, not distinguished by high birth or high position. Our perils are of another kind; we are in danger of being discontented and envious. The workman with thirty shillings a week sometimes envies the foreman with three pounds. The foreman sometimes envies the master; the draper's assistant sometimes envies the head of the firm; the merchant's clerk sometimes envies the merchant. The small manufacturer and the small shopkeeper sometimes envy the great people in their own way of business. The doctor with a poor practice sometimes envies the doctor who attends wealthy people and gets large fees; the lawyer who can hardly afford to keep a clerk sometimes envies the prosperous solicitor and famous barrister. Thank God it is not always so. Indeed, I believe that envy of this kind is far less common than we often imagine. I have long ceased to bring sweeping charges against whole classes of men, if it was ever my foolish habit to bring such charges. It is the people who are proud of their prosperity, and who despise men that are less fortunate than themselves, who think that the less fortunate envy them, just as people who envy the greater prosperity of other men think that the prosperous despise them.

We have seen how sternly James deals with the rich; there is sternness in his dealings with the brother of low degree. He was a compassionate man for real distress, as appears later in the Epistle, but here there is no softness. He does not tell the brother of low degree that he is badly used, that society is hard upon him, that many a poor man deserves to be rich, many an obscure man to be distinguished and famous. Here he expresses no sympathy with the man who is not so prosperous as other men, whose place is among the undistinguished millions of ordinary people. Sympathy? No! That is not his present mood.

'*Let the brother of low degree glory in his high estate.*' There is something manly, something really Christian in that. Do not complain of your want of riches, of your hard work, of your want of distinction. Glory in the greatness of your wealth, and in the greatness of your position as sons of God and heirs of eternal blessedness. Think what you are. The eternal God loves you with as warm a love as that which He has for the richest and most eminent of your Christian brethren. You are as dear to Him as if you had the estates of a duke. You are as dear to Him as if you had in your veins the blood of a long line of noble ancestors. You are as dear to Him as if you were a famous minister, or a great orator, or a great poet. You who are His child, '*glory in your high estate.*' You are poor, but you are not at home. You are on a journey, on your way to the home that God has prepared for you. Even princes do not wear their robes and their crowns while they are travelling, nor do rich men carry their wealth with them. You, too, my poor brother, are rich enough at home. And you are on your way there. Glory in your high estate.

There is a famous passage in Macaulay's *Essay on Milton*, in which, with all the brilliance of his rhetoric, though not without its characteristic defects, he describes the Puritans. 'If their steps were not accompanied by a splendid train of menials, legions of ministering angels had charge over them. Their palaces were houses not made with hands; their diadems crowns of glory which should never fade away. On the rich and the eloquent, on nobles and priests, they looked down with contempt; for they deemed themselves rich in a more precious treasure and eloquent in a more sublime language; nobles by the right of an earlier creation, and priests by the imposition of a mightier hand.'

That is a great passage, with all its imperfections, and if we make one correction it describes the true temper of a Christian man. Contempt, whether for nobles or for priests, whether for the rich or the poor, should never have a place in a Christian heart. The Christian man should '*glory in his high estate*,' but should never despise others. For them, too, though they may not know it, Christ died. They, too, even when unconscious, are encircled by divine love. They, too, are the heirs of an eternal glory. They, too, are among those whom Christ came to seek and to save.

What a different life Christian men and women would live throughout the week if they kept in their thoughts the palaces which are to be their homes, the crowns which they are to wear, the dignity which belongs to them already, and the greater dignity which they may win by the gentle speech, by the courteous manners, the gracious temper, the truthfulness, the uprightness, the industry, the purity which should distinguish them as the sons and daughters of God,—if they would think of all the wealth and glory that are theirs, however humble may be their earthly condition.

I was returning yesterday from Church Stretton, where I had been for a few days' rest. It was a brilliant afternoon, and as we came through Shropshire and North Staffordshire the country seemed perfectly beautiful. When we reached Wolverhampton there was a great contrast. You know the country—huge masses of cinders and black waste upon the mounds; dreary workshops, rows of mean houses, foul with dirt and smoke; the very grass, where it would grow at all, unlovely and dingy. I said, 'What a change!' but then I lifted my eyes, and above all that dreary waste there was a divine glory. In the west the sun was sinking in a sea of flame. The heavy clouds were of rich purple, fringed with fire; lighter clouds, touched with the sun, were of a brilliant orange. It was a vision of transcendent splendour. And that may be a true type of your life. Your earthly condition may be poor, mean, ignoble. But over you too God's heaven is hanging. It is always there,—the sun in its splendour by day, the shining hosts of stars by night; these are the heritage of the brother of low degree, as well as of the rich and the great. Every promise of divine love, every gift of the divine grace, every dignity that belongs to the children of the Most High, every immortal hope,—they are all yours. Live like men whom God has so greatly blessed. '*Glory in your high estate.*'

III

TEMPTATIONS AND TRIALS

'*Blessed is the man that endureth temptation: for when he hath been approved, he shall receive the crown of life, which the Lord promised to them that love him. Let no man say when he is tempted, I am tempted of God: for God cannot be tempted with evil, and he himself tempteth no man: but each man is tempted, when he is drawn away by his own lust, and enticed. Then the lust, when it hath conceived, beareth sin: and the sin, when it is full-grown, bringeth forth death. Be not deceived, my beloved brethren. Every good gift and every perfect boon is from above, coming down from the Father of lights, with whom can be no variation, neither shadow that is cast by turning. Of his own will he brought us forth by the word of truth, that we should be a kind of firstfruits of his creatures.*'—JAMES i. 12-18.

THE style of the writer of this Epistle is energetic and vivid. He is dramatic; he often states great truths in a form which touches on paradox, and so he compels active thought. In this passage a singular effect is produced by the sharply contrasted meaning in which he uses two words to which it would be natural to attribute the same substantial meaning.

'*Blessed is the man that endureth temptation: for when he hath been approved he shall receive the crown of life which the Lord promised to them that love him.*'

That is an excellent reason for the precept we

have already considered; '*count it all joy when ye fall into manifold temptations.*' If the temptations work patience, if by enduring them we win the crown of life, it is possible to rejoice in them. But according to James, to 'fall into temptation' is one thing,—in that we are to rejoice; but to be 'tempted' is quite another thing. God may send temptations, or trials, or troubles on a man: they give him the chance of showing that he trusts perfectly in the Divine Love; that while the Divine Love is left to him, he can be cheerful and grateful, though he suffers the loss of property, of health, of friends, of public honour; of showing that he cares so much for God's authority and God's approval that no inducements are strong enough to prevail upon him to turn aside from the path of integrity; that his chief concern in life is to know more of God, to love God more earnestly, and to make sure of eternal blessedness. God, I say, may send temptations, trials, in order to test our strength and to perfect it; and if we endure them we are to receive the '*crown of life.*' But '*let no man say when he is tempted, I am tempted of God: for God cannot be tempted with evil, and he himself tempteth no man.*' To tempt a man is to induce him to sin. God may send temptations, or troubles, but He never tempts us. '*Be not deceived, my beloved brethren,*' James says further on, '*Every good gift and every perfect boon is from above.*' It is not temptation—in the evil sense of the word—that comes from God, but everything that contributes to the perfection and power and glory of life. '*Every good gift and every perfect boon is from above, coming down from the Father of lights.*' Temptation to sin cannot come from Him.

'*The Father of lights*': that is a striking description of God. God is like the sun who is the centre and chief of all the glories of the visible universe. The sun among the stars is like a father among his children, a prince among his subjects. But the sun of the visible heavens holds no constant place; he rises in the morning and only gradually reaches his meridian splendour, and then he gradually declines and sinks in the west. With God there can be no variation; His splendour is always the splendour of noonday. As the result of what the ancients regarded as the revolution of the spheres, the sun of the visible heavens is sometimes obscured; a shadow is cast upon him; he is eclipsed. But as there is no change in God's own glory, neither can that glory be dimmed by change in His creation; no shadow is cast upon him by any turning. All His gifts are good: He cannot tempt us, for His goodness is unchangeable.

And again, He cannot tempt us, because, as James says, '*He brought us forth by the word of truth,*'—gave us a new life, made us His children by the power of the Christian gospel, '*that we should be a kind of first-fruits of his creatures,*'—a consecrated sacrifice to Himself, like the firstfruits of the ancient law. It would be to defeat His own purpose, if He tempted us to sin.

How then are we to explain 'temptation,' in the evil sense of the word? Where does it come from? Mr. Mayor, in his admirable commentary on this Epistle, says that we have here the first attempt at an analysis of temptation from the Christian point of view, and adds that it may be compared with that given by Bishop Butler in his *Analogy*.[1] But Butler deals with the subject as a philosopher; James deals with it practically as a Jewish prophet or a Christian teacher. James's account of 'temptation' as distinguished from 'trial'—of temptation in its evil sense,—amounts to this; no outward circumstances constitute a temptation to sin, apart from some irregular, uncontrolled desire, or what James calls '*lust*,' in a man's own heart. The 'lust' may be for riches, or for ease, or for personal distinction, or for power, or for personal display, or for the pleasures of eating or of drinking. But there must be some irregular or uncontrolled desire in a man's own heart. If not, outward circumstances can never constitute a temptation to sin. So that a man is tempted when he is drawn away from the right path by '*his own lust, and enticed*.' The inward desire or lust meets the outward opportunity which entices him; and in James's vigorous imaginative way they are married, and together they become the parents of sin; and this sin, he says, '*when it is full-grown, bringeth forth death*.'

It is not God that tempts us to sin, and no

[1] Butler: *Analogy*, Part I., capp. 4 and 5. Mayor: pp. 175-178.

external circumstances can become a temptation to sin, apart from something in ourselves. Christ, you remember, said, 'The prince of the world cometh, and he hath nothing in me.'[1] 'Sin,' to quote Mr. Mayor again, 'is the result of the surrender of the will to the solicitation of lust or desire, instead of the guidance of reason;' or, as I would rather say, of conscience and of God. 'In itself, the desire may be natural, and innocent: it is when the man resolves to gratify it against what he feels to be the law of duty'—and the will of God,—'that he becomes guilty of sin, even before he carries out his resolve in act.'[2]

We, indeed, do not ascribe to God our temptations to sin; we ascribe them sometimes to circumstances, sometimes to the people with whom we are living. No doubt there are some of us who are so constituted that our circumstances are a constant provocation to sin, and if we cannot help our circumstances, we must look to God for strength to resist the temptation. But if our circumstances are of our own choice if we could change them to-morrow, we have no right to ask God for strength or defence; He will leave us to the result of our choice. No doubt some of us have companions and friends that are a constant provocation to sin; but here again, if our companions and friends are of our own choice, if we have allowed ourselves to drift into friendship with them, when we might have had friends of another kind; if we associate ourselves with people who

[1] John xiv. 30.

[2] Mayor, p. 51.

have no religious earnestness, because they are richer, or more amusing, than others to whom religion is a supreme reality; if in this way we voluntarily live in the society of men who do nothing to deepen our love for Christ, and to increase our earnestness in His service, then we have no right to ask God for grace to keep us right; if we do ask, He will not hear us.

And further, there are certain habits of life which render us accessible to temptation to sin; most men have, I suppose, learnt this. They know what those habits are. The habits in themselves may be perfectly innocent, but with people of particular temperaments they are not only perilous but fatal. Nothing, for example, can be more innocent than the reading of good works of fiction. With many of us they are not only a refreshment and a delight, but a positive aid to intellectual and moral culture. But there are some who, if they read works of fiction at all, read them to excess; they lose their taste for reading of a graver kind, become so absorbed that they neglect plain duties, are withdrawn from interest in the life of their homes, and become irritable and impatient. Some men, again, cannot drink at all without being in danger of drinking immoderately. Even moderate drinking,—I mean moderate in amount,—has a disastrous effect on some men; it brightens them for a time, but then it dulls them; it makes them quick, and alert, and kindly for an hour or two, and then it leaves them desponding and sluggish.

But let us return to James's account of what we should call trials as distinguished from temptations: '*Blessed is the man that endureth temptation* (trial), *for when he hath been approved, he shall receive the crown of life.*' The definite promise of the crown of life to those who love Christ does not occur in any of the four Gospels; the promise is perhaps one of those sayings of our Lord which were preserved by tradition, though not recorded by any of the four Evangelists. It is to the man who *endures* trial, and who comes out of it *approved*, that the crown of life is promised. Let there be no mistake. It is not mere suffering that secures for a man the great future, but the devout, trustful, patient endurance of suffering. It is not the mere trial that makes the blessedness certain, but the standing of the test; some men are tried and found worthless; it is not the cross that gives us the crown, but the endurance of the cross for Christ's sake, despising the shame. One of the thieves, who hung on a cross by the very side of Christ, was impenitent to the last, and to him the cross has brought no glory either in the memory of man or in the judgment of God.

There is a common delusion on this subject. No one supposes that because a man is appointed to great and difficult duties, he necessarily wins great honour. The having to discharge great duties sometimes involves a man in public shame: it is the way in which he discharges his duties, not the mere fact that he has them to discharge that brings the glory.

And so it is not present suffering that makes future blessedness secure; it is not the being tried that makes the crown of life certain, but the manner in which we meet the trial. It is not enough for a gun to be sent to the proof-house; some guns burst that are sent there.

Are we enduring our trials—coming out of them with honour? Does every fresh trial give fresh proof of our fidelity to God, and increase it? There are the vexations and annoyances by which many young people are irritated as they approach manhood and womanhood,—ceasing to be children, but not yet men and women; or even if they are men and women, their parents cannot quite realise it. Are you going through these trials with a light and cheerful and generous heart? Are you mastering that disposition to self-assertion which is one of your chief dangers, showing affection and respect to those who, as you think, do not treat you with all the consideration that your growing years might claim? Are those of you who are just coming into contact with the roughnesses of life, who find your work irksome and monotonous, your companions selfish and unsympathetic,—are you firmly resisting tendencies to idleness; are you keeping yourselves well in hand, putting your whole strength into your work, whether you like it or not; treating the people about you as you wish they would treat you, instead of returning the evil treatment which you sometimes receive from them? If you have an irritable master over you, do you keep your temper; if he is unreasonable and grasping, do you care for his interests though he seems to care very little for yours? If you are placed over others and they are unpunctual and careless, stubborn in doing their work in their own way, and hard to persuade that there is a better way,—are you rough or gentle with them? Do you make them worse by your violence, or better by a firmness tempered with consideration and kindness? If you are a tradesman and times are hard with you, do you resist the strong inducements to save yourself at the cost of other people; to stretch a point in your own favour, as people say, which means in more exact speech to cheat another man for your own advantage? If your income is sinking, are you trying hard to sink your expenses? If you are in bad health, are you keeping a sweet and kindly temper? If your mind is dull, do you bear without resentment the annoyance which bright and active-minded people are apt to inflict, sometimes very mercilessly, on people who are not so clever as themselves? If you are alert, quick, brilliant, do you avoid the miserable vice of treating other people as though they were fools? If you are prosperous, are you avoiding the temptation to insolence and display; and are you mastering the fierce passion for laying up wealth? If you are surrounded by people who have no religious faith and make a mock of it, do you with calmness and unflinching courage maintain your own testimony to the authority of God and the love and power of the Lord

Jesus Christ? If you are assailed yourself by keen intellectual doubts about the environments of Divine revelation, do you retain through all uncertainty your vivid impression of the perfect grace, the majestic righteousness, the transcendent moral and religious glory of Him, whose words and deeds are recorded in the four Gospels? Are you trusting in Him perfectly for salvation; are you keeping all His commandments? Is there any secret satisfaction in the prospect which your doubts suggest of release from obligations which are imposed by faith, any weariness at the great tasks to which we are called by our relations to God and by the prospect of immortality? The question, I repeat, is not whether we are being tried, but how we are standing the trial,—whether as the result of the test we are approved.

To reinforce the infirmity of human resolution, to rekindle the fire of those Divine affections which the rough winds of this world so often extinguish, look forward to the issues of faithfulness on the one hand, and of unfaithfulness on the other. Yield to temptation, commit sin, and sin will bring forth death, eternal death,—the loss of the eternal life and peace and power and perfection and blessedness to which you are destined in Christ. Endure the trial, come out of it victoriously, and from the hands of Christ will come the victor's wreath, the eternal life of the saints in glory.

There are some who disparage the moral worth of

the great revelation which Christ has given of the future beyond death; forgetting that it was largely by the revelation of judgment to come, with eternal life as its issue on the one hand, and eternal death on the other, that the Christian faith accomplished its triumphs. And if there were no future, or if we knew nothing of it, there would be infinite discouragement in the pursuit of perfection. Think what it would mean; a man through protracted suffering might reach a high degree of moral excellence, and then what had been won at so great a price would perish; just when it was complete it would disappear; when the last touch of grace was given to it, when it had been disciplined to perfect strength, it would all be dissolved and would pass away. But we are told that the memory of it would remain, that the great example, the conspicuous righteousness, would survive in the grateful admiration of the human race, and that the lofty fidelity of the transient life would contribute to the moral advancement of mankind. That would be something; and if there were nothing more, we should have to dwell on it, and to make the most of it. But for myself, though my heart thrills to the heroic strain of the old Stoicism, and to the echoes of it in the writings of some modern ethical philosophers, it would seem, as I have said, infinitely discouraging, if after a man had endured loss, pain, dishonour, in his loyalty to conscience, and in his desire to be perfect and entire, lacking in nothing, the moral perfection thus achieved perished at death, and survived only in the memory of those who had watched its gradual approach to completion. What painter would have the courage and the endurance to devote several months of his life to a painting, in which his genius was to reveal all its splendour, if he knew that at the moment the work was finished, when the last brush of varnish had been laid on, it would be destroyed by fire, leaving only the remembrance of it to survive in the minds of those who had visited his studio and seen it in the successive stages of its progress? And if every palace, every temple, when it was completed, when the last stroke of the chisel had been given to the carving, when it had been enriched with all beautiful and precious things, were destined to be destroyed by earthquake or shattered by storm,—if from this doom there were no escape,—what architect, what prince, what church, would care to spend genius and treasure in erecting it? And if the moral nobleness and beauty which require a patience and a suffering beyond what any artist ever had to consecrate to the expression of his imagination on canvas, which impose a severer strain on the moral energies of men, and involve a greater cost, than the erection of the most stately buildings that have ever commanded the wonder and veneration of mankind,—if these were to perish as soon as they were perfected, the moral courage of most men would be paralysed, and they would be content to live a life of compromise and ease.

Desperate indeed would be our condition if the

great hope were not ours. When the elastic energy of youth declines,—and with some it declines very soon,—when the passion and energy which make hardship itself exhilarating, begin to sink, many a man would renounce the attempt to achieve a perfect righteousness, unless he knew that the righteousness would be eternal. For some of you life is a very troubled sea; storm after storm breaks upon you; the winds are fierce, the waves run high; and if it were certain that sooner or later the ship would run upon an iron-bound coast at night, or be destroyed in mid-ocean by the fury of the tempest, struck by the lightning, shattered by heavy seas, I do not know what heart or courage you would have to fight the winds and the waves any longer. It is the port which, by the divine help, you are sure of making; it is the land of eternal sunlight and peace to which at last, through God's defence, you are sure to come, that makes it supremely worth while to oppose to all difficulties a stubborn and invincible endurance.

The '*crown of life*,' the victor's wreath, is for those who have endured temptation. The perfect life itself, which God will give, is the crown which we hope for. Just as the flowers are the crown, when we speak of a crown of flowers, or the laurel, when we speak of a crown of laurel. Life—life with clearer vision than is possible to us in this world; life sensitive to more subtle and more ravishing harmonies; life with diviner buoyancy and vigour; life with more intense affections; life with wider horizons of thought; life with new and unhoped-for possibilities of righteousness; life with the capacity for closer friendships with the saintly spirits of the city of God; life with loftier raptures of adoration; life with profounder awe in the presence of God's majesty; life with the blessedness of a more intimate communion with the peace and love of God—life is what we hope for.

Not the shining palaces of the heavenly city, but the regal spirit; not the golden harps of the blessed, but the perfect music of the moral and spiritual harmony which comes from being filled with God; not the white robes, but the stainless spiritual purity; not the wreath of honour, but the Divine approval of our righteousness, of which the wreath is but the gracious symbol. The higher, larger, purer life is what we hope for; and this is what God has promised us. He promises it to those who love Him and who have endured temptation; for it is by the endurance of temptation in the power of love for Christ that the capacity for receiving that life in its amplest measure and noblest perfection is enlarged and perfected.

IV

HEARING AND DOING

'*Ye know this, my beloved brethren. But let every man be swift to hear, slow to speak, slow to wrath: for the wrath of man worketh not the righteousness of God. Wherefore putting away all filthiness and overflowing of malice, receive with meekness the implanted word, which is able to save your souls. But be ye doers of the word, and not hearers only, deluding your own selves. For if any one is a hearer of the word, and not a doer, he is like unto a man beholding his natural face in a mirror: for he beholdeth himself, and goeth away, and straightway forgetteth what manner of man he was. But he that looketh into the perfect law, the law of liberty, and so continueth, being not a hearer that forgetteth, but a doer that worketh, this man shall be blessed in his doing. If any man thinketh himself to be religious, while he bridleth not his tongue but deceiveth his heart, this man's religion is vain. Pure religion and undefiled before our God and Father is this, to visit the fatherless and widows in their affliction, and to keep himself unspotted from the world.*'—JAMES i. 19-27.

THE truths which James has stated in the preceding passage were very elementary truths. The Christian people to whom he was writing might need to be reminded of them, but they knew them well. They knew that God would not tempt any of them to sin; they knew that every good gift came from Him, and that He could not do them any evil. They knew that He could not tempt them to sin, for if He tempted them to sin it would be to defeat His own purpose. For '*of His own will He had brought them forth by the word of truth, that they should be a kind of first-fruits of His creatures*;' consecrated to Himself like the first-fruits under the ancient Jewish law. And so James begins this new paragraph with the words, '*Ye know this, my beloved brethren.*'

Yes, they knew it; but it was not quite clear that their knowledge influenced life and conduct. And so James proceeds to give them some practical precepts, which we shall see are very closely connected with what he has already said. He has said that God of His own will '*brought them forth*,'—gave them life, a new and divine life,—'*by the word of truth.*' He will exhort them presently to continue to receive that word, for if they do not continue to receive it they cannot be saved; but he gives them first some subordinate precepts which lead up to that. '*Ye know this*'; know all that I have said about temptation and about your receiving life through the power of God's word. But '*let every man be swift to hear, slow to speak.*'

I have sometimes recommended you to underline or to copy out every precept in the New Testament, which you have never thought of obeying. Perhaps some of you might begin here. I think it likely that this precept is precisely the one which some of you for your salvation need to remember and obey. '*Be swift to hear, slow to speak.*' You have thought about other divine words,—divine words concerning the love of God and the Christian salvation, or the power and grace of the Holy Spirit, but somehow you are very little the better. Now, suppose that you lay to heart these words. Perhaps, as I have said, they are the very words which, if they were only implanted in your heart and took root there, would save you. '*Be swift to hear*'—ready to listen to what other men say; '*slow to speak*'—not eager to talk yourselves.

There are some people who are always talking. They cannot think, and it is a relief to them to hear the sound of their own voices. Just as women who are in ill-health find a welcome relief in sewing or knitting, and sew or knit just to pass the time, there are some people who find relief in talking; and by their incessant talking they disable themselves from thinking. They also disable themselves from listening. They lose the power of grasping the real meaning of anything serious that is said to them. Their minds are like reservoirs with a large leak and a small supply of water; everything that comes into them runs off at once, and they are always empty. Incessant talking, without careful and earnest listening, makes them utterly frivolous, reduces them almost to a state of idiocy. And further, this habit prevents them from listening even to God's word and from thinking about it. They are not accustomed to listen or to think, and so when the divine word comes to them they cannot really listen to it, and they cannot brood over it.

There are, however, people of quite another description, who might save their souls if they would be swift to hear and slow to speak; very clever people who really know a great deal; keen observers who have something to say, but who are ruined by their incessant talking. They learn a great deal from reading, but they never think, and they never give themselves a chance of learning anything in conversation. Whenever they read anything in a book or in a newspaper that they suppose will make good talk, they seem to take a note of it, and they use it on the first opportunity. They have opinions on everything; they criticise everybody. If a man is building a house for himself, they explain to him how much better he might do it. If they are travelling by train, they make it quite clear that the traffic manager does not know his business, and that they could arrange the hours of the trains very much more effectively and conveniently. They are much wiser about the management of municipal affairs than all the members of the Town Council put together, and much wiser about the management of schools than all the members of the School Board. They are always talking and always lecturing. They have immeasurable self-confidence; it never seems to occur to them that it is possible for them to learn anything from anybody; they sometimes become intolerably arrogant. Now that attitude, that temper of mind in relation to men, is unfriendly to receiving the '*implanted word*' of God. '*Be swift to hear, slow to speak*'; this surely is not a difficult precept to obey.

It is so hard to talk to any purpose; it is so easy not to talk at all.

But there are some people indeed that are very '*slow to speak*,' who are very far from obeying the precept. They are not '*swift to hear*;' they are sluggishly indifferent to the people about them; they do not speak, because they are absorbed in themselves, and therefore they do not listen. That is an evil temper of another kind, and also needs correction.

The vice which James condemns is a vice which appears in conversation of all kinds, and he meant to condemn it in every form; but I suppose he meant specially to condemn it when shown in religious conversation. Among us, indeed, this is not a very common fault; in fact, our fault lies in quite another direction. But even among us there are people who are much too unwilling to listen and much too eager to speak about religion; their religious talk flows in one wearisome monotonous stream. There is very little of anything in it; they talk too much to think much, to know much, to feel much, or to do much. It is talk which has no root below the lips; there is no sign that it comes from the depths of life. And the mischief is that these people often think that they are living very religiously because they talk very religiously. The truth is that the strength which ought to go into life is wasted in talk; the steam blows off instead of doing its work. They need to form the habit of listening, if they are to receive more of the divine word.

'*Be swift to hear, slow to speak, slow to wrath.*' People who talk a great deal are very apt to heat themselves by talking: they get excited, they provoke contradiction and discussion, and then their temper rises; that is true, whatever the talk is about. And it is often true, unhappily, when the talk is about religion. Indeed there are men who mistake heat and passion in the maintenance of their own religious opinions, for fidelity to God and earnestness in God's service. They are intolerant. People who maintain traditional beliefs are intolerant in defending them; people who reject traditional beliefs are intolerant in assailing them; the intolerance is as great on the one side as on the other. But '*the wrath of man,*' James says, '*worketh not the righteousness of God.*' Your heated feeling, though it may be created by what you think is a good cause, does not make you a better servant of God or of man; it contributes nothing to your own righteousness, it provokes other people to sin.

And now James comes to his great precept: '*Wherefore putting away all filthiness and overflowing of malice, receive with meekness the implanted word which is able to save your souls.*' He means that to receive God's word you must not have any unkindly, any malignant feelings towards men; the rising up, the '*overflowing of malice*' defiles you. It is moral filth which excludes you from the presence of God, just as ceremonial uncleanness excluded men from the ancient temple. You cannot be in a right relation to God while you have angry and unfriendly feelings towards other men. While you are arrogant and contemptuous in your spirit towards them, you cannot receive His word. Putting away then all self-assertion, all hostility, all ill-feeling and all uncleanliness towards men, '*receive with meekness*' the divine word. The spirit of gentleness and kindliness towards others is necessary if we are rightly to receive the word of God. Our Lord said that if, when we have brought our gift to the altar, we remember that our brother has any just complaint against us, we are to leave our gift before the altar and first go to our brother and remove his resentment, and then offer our gift. James says here that we are to become meek and kindly towards men; to put aside our sense of self-importance, our irritation, our unfriendliness, and so to receive the word of God.

Receive with meekness '*the implanted word, which is able to save your souls.*'

'*The implanted word.*' It is a seed which has life in it. It takes root where it is received. It springs up and bears fruit in righteous and holy living. It '*is able,*' James says, '*to save your souls.*' Do you all remember this fact? This word, of which he is speaking, is a word from God; it declares a truth,—a truth so great, of such importance to the moral and spiritual life of men, that God has thought it worth while to speak it. It rebukes a sin, the rebuke is from God; it enforces a duty, a duty enforced by God's authority; it contains a promise which God is ready to fulfil; it warns against a danger from which God desires to protect you; it is '*able to save your souls*,' and was spoken that your souls might be saved. God speaks it: that is a reason for receiving it. It '*is able to save your souls*,'—has that wonderful power in it; and that is another reason for receiving it. I am certain that in the conduct of life we do not give the divine word its right place; we want to be saved from our sins, but we forget that the divine word is able to save us,—the divine Word concerning the love which moved God to give us His Son that we might have eternal life,—concerning the death of His Son for the remission of sins, and His resurrection from the dead; concerning the necessity of being born again; concerning the power and grace of the Holy Spirit; concerning the willingness of God to listen to our prayers; concerning the presence of Christ among us when we are met together in Christ's name; concerning the defence and support which Christ gives to those who trust Him; concerning Christ's authority over human life; concerning riches and poverty; concerning the honour which comes from men; concerning the claims of other men on our service; concerning the government of the tongue and the government of our thought; concerning judgment by works; concerning future blessedness and glory; concerning the indignation and wrath, tribulation and anguish, which are to come upon every man that doeth evil; concerning the loss—the eternal loss—which even the saved will suffer if they are not faithful to Christ, for they will be saved 'but so as through fire.' These are the divine words which are '*able to save your souls*'; you will not be saved unless they are so received as to become moral and spiritual forces, inspiring, sustaining, shaping life and conduct. Earnest desire to become better men and women, endeavours to become better, self-discipline, will all fail, except as they are sustained and directed by the power of the divine word. The divine word is able to save your souls; that is why it is preached in this place, and why you are asked to be devout and earnest readers of Holy Scripture, in which the divine word, as spoken and revealed by prophets and apostles and the Lord Jesus Christ Himself, is contained.

The divine word '*is able to save your souls*'; incessant talking, even about religious truth, will do nothing for you, nor hot zeal for truth. The rejection of error, passionate hostility against error, is not enough. The word, the divine word, must be so received as to take root in life, and therefore, we should be '*swift to hear, slow to speak, slow to wrath*,' and should '*receive the word with meekness*.'

And now James passes to a second precept. Those Christian people deceive themselves and imperil their eternal salvation who do not care to hear the word of God. But it is not enough for us to be *hearers*, we must be *doers*. Plainly, however, we must be hearers before we can be doers. The word must be listened to; its meaning must be discovered by earnest thought.

It must be so dwelt upon as to have the chance of exerting all its power upon us; else we cannot do it. But doing is necessary as well as hearing.

I suppose that there are many people who have a delight in hearing fervent, picturesque, animating, impressive preaching, and in reading religious books which seem to surround the soul with a certain ethereal atmosphere, but who are not '*doers of the word*.' They listen for the pleasure of listening. They like to have their religious emotions excited; emotional excitement of that kind is as pleasant as the excitement produced by pathetic poetry, by great eloquence, or by the theatre. And there is this further attraction in it: people suppose that to have their religious emotions excited is a sign of goodness, and that it does them good. And so whenever a preacher wins a reputation for great power, there are some people who try to hear him; they crowd revival services; they go to religious conventions; or, if they are young, they attend the meetings of Religious Endeavour Societies; they want to hear and to be impressed. If a preacher has the kind of power which moves half his congregation to tears, he has an irresistible charm for them. If he has a triumphant and exulting temper, and excites those who hear him to great joy, he is also attractive. What they want, I say, is to hear and to be impressed. Others, again, but not so many, find great delight in the vigorous thought, in the clearness and definiteness and in the intellectual force with which the truth is preached; and indeed the truth itself interests them as an object of intellectual speculation. But when the book which charms them is closed, and when the service, the convention, the meeting, which excited them, is over, they are no better than they were before. They have been deeply moved by what they have heard of the love of Christ, but it cannot be said of them next day that the love of Christ constrains them 'because they thus judge, that one died for all, therefore all died; and He died for all, that they which live should no longer live to themselves, but unto Him who for their sakes died and rose again.'[1]

They were thrilled while listening to a vivid representation of the blessedness and glory of the great life to come, but next day they seem no more eager to lay up treasure in heaven than they were before, and they are just as eager for earthly riches and honour. They were awed by what they heard about every man receiving at the Judgment the things done in the body, but next day the thought of the Judgment does not make them more just, more truthful, more pure, more self-sacrificing. They listen with delight to some keen and vigorous assault on vanity or self-conceit, on pride, on ambition, on indolence, on the habit of criticising others. But the next day they are just the same,—just as conceited, just as proud, just as ambitious, just as indolent, just as ready to pronounce judgment on others as they ever

[1] 2 Cor. v. 14, 15.

were. They are '*hearers of the word, not doers.*' They delude themselves; they think that because they have strong religious emotions they are religious. Religious emotion may help us to be religious; but to be actually religious is to be under the power of God always and everywhere. They think that they have faith, because great divine truths interest, charm, excite them; but to have faith is to be actually governed by these truths in thought and in feeling, in our plan of life, in the objects for which we live, in our work, and in our actions. They think that they are good men because they are fascinated by the perfection to which Christ calls us; but to be good is to be actually moving towards that perfection. They think that they are excellent Christians because it is a delight to them to hear about Christ; but to be a Christian is to keep His commandments; they are '*hearers only, deluding their own selves.*'

And '*if any one is a hearer of the word, and not a doer, he is like unto a man beholding his natural face in a mirror:*' like a man who looks at himself for a moment without any particular purpose in looking, and turns away at once; and, as James says, '*straightway forgetteth what manner of man he was.*' His face may be so pale as to indicate great weakness; but he has just glanced and he hardly notices it and at once forgets. Or there may be spots on it which are signs of some disease; but they leave no lasting impression on his mind: they pass out of his memory as soon as he has ceased to look.

'*But he that looketh into the perfect law, the law of liberty*,'—bends over it with a thoughtful and earnest desire to discover what it contains,—'*and so continueth*,'—keeps on examining it, because he wants to understand it, to remember it, and do it,—'*being not a hearer that forgetteth, but a doer that worketh, this man shall be blessed in his doing*.' He discovers from his close and earnest examination of the divine word what he ought to be: he discovers what he is. He listens, he reads, with a view to life and practice; the word saves him.

That is a fine phrase—'*the law of liberty*.' It is one of those paradoxes in which James delights. It is a law, and the very essence of law is to impose constraint; to require a man to follow a line of conduct chosen, not by himself, but by a power above him. And in the Christian Gospel there is a law; a law requiring severer sacrifices and a higher perfection than the law of Old Testament times, and than any of the ethical systems of Paganism. But the Christian gospel is '*a law of liberty*'; for while imposing these obligations, it gives the heart to obey them. It requires us to love God; but it so reveals the love of God for us, as to kindle the love it requires. It requires us to love our neighbour as ourselves; but it draws us into such intimate fellowship and union with Christ that His love for men becomes ours. It requires us to care more for doing

God's will and securing His approval than for riches, honour, ease, and all the transient pleasures of this life; but it reveals such transcendent blessedness in God that the heart which receives the revelation finds in God its supreme attraction, and innumerable saints have counted as nothing all the wealth and splendours and delights of this world, in their eagerness to lay up treasure in heaven, and to win 'the honour that cometh from God alone.'[1] It requires us to avoid all sin; but it inspires an abhorrence of sin so as to make us hate that which it forbids. Tell a thief not to steal,—and the law is a restraint on him. But if the law could make him an honest man, the law which forbids theft would be a '*law of liberty*': he would no longer want to steal. Tell a drunkard not to drink,—the law is a restraint on him; he may try to obey it, but to obey will be very irksome. But if the law could take away his love of drink, it would be a '*law of liberty*': he would keep it because he liked to keep it. It is a law that a mother should care for her children; if she does not, she is a wicked woman. But to nearly all mothers it is a '*law of liberty*': it requires her to do the very thing she delights in doing. It is a Christian law to speak the truth; but the Christian under the power of Christ abhors lying; it is a '*law of liberty*.' It is a Christian law to pray; but the Christian longs to pray: it is a '*law of liberty*.' It is a Christian law that a man should `ttend worship;

[1] John v. 44

but the Christian longs to attend worship: it is a '*law of liberty.*' It is a Christian law that a man should contribute generously to the relief of human suffering and the rescue of men from sin; but a Christian finds his delight in doing this, is eager to do it: it is a '*law of liberty.*'

The Christian gospel is a law of liberty because it creates in the hearts of those who perfectly receive it the disposition and the power to obey it. If we have reason to fear that this disposition to obey the Divine law has not been created in us, if the will of God is still felt to be an irksome restraint, if we are not gaining power to keep it, we have reason to fear that we have not received the gospel. At first, and for a time, we shall have to do our duty against our inclination; but gradually the power of the Christian gospel will change our inclination, and though some Christian duties may continue for a long time to be difficult, they will gradually become our delight.

Let us pass on. '*If any man thinketh himself to be religious, while he bridleth not his tongue but deceiveth his heart, this man's religion is vain.*' James means that if a man supposes he is observing all his religious duties, and therefore supposes that he is bridling his tongue, while yet he is not bridling it, this man's religion is vain. No man, that is, can be so ignorant as not to know that if he is to be religious he must bridle his tongue; that is an obvious and elementary truth. But some men deceive themselves; they think that they are bridling their tongues and are not doing it; their religion '*is vain.*' Evidently sins of the tongue were very common and very flagrant among these Jewish Christians. James began the paragraph we are considering by charging them to be '*swift to hear and slow to speak,*' and he returns in this verse to the same necessity of keeping the tongue under restraint. But there is so much more in the Epistle about the government of the tongue that I will not dwell on this passage at greater length.

James has used the word *religious*, and after his manner he catches up the word and dwells upon it. Religion, '*pure religion,*' '*undefiled*' religion, the religion which is acceptable to God,—what is it? The word he uses, and which is translated '*religion,*' has a very definite meaning. It does not mean the inward faith and love and awe which constitute the spirit of religion, and apart from which everything else that calls itself religion is worthless. The word '*religion*' in this place stands for very much what we mean when we speak of ritual or ceremonial,—the visible outward expression of inward faith and awe and love. The Jews—and James was writing to Jewish Christians—would call a man 'religious' who was very attentive to these external religious observances, who kept the great religious feasts, who said his prayers at the proper hours every day, who avoided ceremonial uncleanness, who was careful to meet every external demand of the Jewish law. Quite another word would be used to describe a righteous man, a devout man, a pious man. What James says is, that the outward ceremonial, the visible ritual, of the Christian faith consists in visiting '*the fatherless and widows in their affliction*,' and in keeping ourselves '*unspotted from the world*.'

It is one of the most beautiful conceptions in the New Testament; the ritual of the Christian faith is in doing works of mercy, and in keeping ourselves from being stained by the world. We serve God, not by offering costly sacrifices on His altars, but by relieving the necessities of the poor; not by appearing before Him in vestments of stainless white, but in keeping ourselves '*unspotted from the world*.'

The words need no comment, their beauty and charm are wonderful. I will make only one observation. I think it possible, at least, that James meant that it will help to keep us '*unspotted from the world*' if we visit the poor and the sorrowful in order to comfort and relieve them. But we must do it ourselves. Writing a cheque, putting a five-pound note into a collection-box, is better than doing nothing; but all experience shows that one of the surest methods of checking worldliness, of keeping ourselves from the worldly spirit and temper and from worldly habits, is '*to visit the fatherless and widows in their affliction*,'—to carry our own personal sympathy into the homes of sorrow.

There are many people who seem to think that James is a great upholder of the claims of morality as against the claims of religion; that he cares more for right conduct than he does for right thinking. Such persons can hardly have read this part of the Epistle; or, if they have ever read it, they must be like the forgetful hearer of whom he writes; they cannot have caught even a faint glimpse of his meaning. They say that he puts the whole emphasis of his exhortation on *doing*. Yes, but on doing what? Doing the word,—the word of God. For a morality that does not rest on the divine word, whatever may be its worth, James has nothing good to say. He does not teach us that if we are honest men, truthful men, kindly men, we shall be saved, no matter whether we receive the word of God and do it or not. He says that it is the word of God that is able to save our souls, and we must not merely be hearers of it; we must think of it, brood over it, let it take root in our hearts, and become doers of it, if we are to be blessed. Right thinking is important for the sake of right doing, but doing can never be wholly right which is not inspired and directed by reverence for God's authority, by delight in God's law, and by an intense desire to win His approval. The doing that James insists upon is the kind of doing that comes from hearing,—from hearing the word of God, every word that God has spoken, and from taking it into our own life.

V

RESPECT OF PÉRSONS

'*My brethren, hold not the faith of our Lord Jesus Christ, the Lord of glory, with respect of persons. For if there come into your synagogue a man with a gold ring, in fine clothing, and there come in also a poor man in vile clothing; and ye have regard to him that weareth the fine clothing, and say, Sit thou here in a good place; and ye say to the poor man, Stand thou there, or sit under my footstool; are ye not divided in your own mind, and become judges with evil thoughts? Hearken, my beloved brethren; did not God choose them that are poor as to the world to be rich in faith, and heirs of the kingdom which He promised to them that love him? But ye have dishonoured the poor man. Do not the rich oppress you, and themselves drag you before the judgment-seats? Do not they blaspheme the honourable name by the which ye are called? Howbeit if ye fulfil the royal law, according to the scripture, Thou shalt love thy neighbour as thyself, ye do well: but if ye have respect of persons, ye commit sin, being convicted by the law as trangressors. For whosoever shall keep the whole law, and yet stumble in one point, he is become guilty of all. For he that said, Do not commit adultery, said also, Do not kill. Now if thou dost not commit adultery, but killest, thou art become a trangressor of the law. So speak ye, and so do, as men that are to be judged by a law of liberty. For judgment is without mercy to him that hath shewed no mercy: mercy glorieth against judgment.*'—JAMES ii. 1-13.

THE Jewish Christians for whom this Epistle was chiefly intended, had received the Christian gospel, but their religious thought and temper were still largely controlled by the traditions of their race.

Their assemblies for religious instruction and worship were still called synagogues, and I suppose that the customs and organisation of the synagogue were preserved almost unchanged in the Church. The great majority of the Christian Jews were poor men. Most of the wealthy Jews,—and there was a great deal of wealth among the Jews in that part of Asia,—were bitterly hostile to the Christian faith, and persecuted cruelly those who acknowledged Jesus of Nazareth as the Messiah. Throughout the Epistle the rich as a class are described as the enemies of the Christian Church, and James denounces them in very much the same temper as that in which the ancient Psalmists denounced the heathen, the enemies of the elect race.

And yet James had heard that in the Christian synagogues the poor were treated with contemptuous discourtesy, and the wealthy with ostentatious demonstrations of respect. What a vivid and picturesque description he gives of their un-Christian manners! A stranger comes in with a gold ring on his finger, wearing a bright, fresh-looking, handsome robe. His appearance creates a sensation among the poor people who are met for worship. It is not often that a rich man appears among them. Two or three of them who are sitting in the pleasantest and most honourable seats, rise at once and offer him a place. Then another stranger comes in, dressed poorly and squalidly; he is told to stand where he can; or, if he prefers it, he can sit on the floor.

This is what James calls '*having respect of persons*,'—an offence which is frequently and sternly condemned in the Old Testament scriptures. To have '*respect of persons*' is to treat them not according to their just claims, but according to their position and their external circumstances. The word which James uses, strictly interpreted, means, as Mr. Mayor says,[1] to take the outside surface for the reality, the mask for the man. James says that for Christians to make this difference between the rich and the poor is to be '*divided*' in their '*own mind*.' It is inconsistent with their Christian faith; it shows that while they professed to have received, and may really have received, what the Christian Gospel has revealed concerning the love of God for all mankind, and concerning the glory, honour, and immortality to which the poor, as well as the rich, are destined in Christ, they are still largely under the power of what is called 'this present evil world.' They have become '*judges with evil thoughts*,'—treating men with honour and dishonour on false grounds. '*Hearken, my beloved brethren*'; he goes on to say, '*Did not God choose them that are poor as to the world to be rich in faith, and heirs of the kingdom which he promised to them that love him?*' He means that there is a much larger proportion of the poor than of the rich among those who have received the Christian salvation. Their poverty did not repel God's grace; '*but ye have dishonoured the poor man*.' On the other

[1] Mayor, p. 73.

hand, the rich,—not all the rich, but the rich as a class,—'*oppress you, and themselves drag you before the judgment-seats.*' They blaspheme the name of Christ into which ye were baptized. What reason have you as Christians, for showing special honour to a stranger simply because his dress and ornaments indicate that he is wealthy? Then follows a sentence which is perhaps ironical.[1] If indeed in treating the rich stranger with this extreme courtesy you are not displaying a coarse and vulgar and un-Christian respect for his wealth, but are only fulfilling '*the royal law, according to the scripture, Thou shalt love thy neighbour as thyself*'; if you want to be even more careful in fulfilling the law in your treatment of the rich, because the rich as a class are your enemies,—if this is the real reason why you show the rich stranger so much consideration, '*ye do well; but if ye have respect of persons, ye commit sin.*'

The principal and enduring ground on which James rests his protest against this contempt of the poor,—simply because they are poor,—and this honouring of the wealthy,—simply because they are wealthy,—is given in the first verse of the chapter. '*My brethren, hold not the faith of our Lord Jesus Christ, the Lord of Glory, with respect of persons.*' In the presence of the Lord Jesus Christ, in whom you have seen the very glory of God, all those distinctions of wealth and social position by which men

[1] Mayor, however, holds that the ironical use of the phrase is found in ver. 19, but that here it is used 'simply.' Mayor, p. 85.

are separated from each other, disappear. In Him you have an eternal wealth, compared with which all earthly riches are worthless ; an eternal glory, which makes the most dazzling earthly splendours pale and dim. The true corrective of these false judgments of men on the ground of their wealth and their poverty is to be found in Christ.

The vehemence and solemnity with which James urges his protest indicate that he was not thinking merely of the contemptuous discourtesy shown to the poor and the excessive consideration shown to the rich in the Christian synagogues, but of the spirit and habit of mind which this evil conduct revealed. He is protesting against an un-Christian estimate of the importance and value of mere material wealth,—an estimate which leads to the disregard of the duty of honouring and loving all men. The protest is as much needed in England to-day as it was among the Jews in the heart of Asia eighteen hundred years ago. As M. de Tocqueville pointed out in his famous book on America, to attach an excessive importance to material wealth is one of the great perils of democratic communities. And as European countries are becoming more democratic, the soundness of his judgment is receiving strong confirmation.

To treat material wealth with indifference and as though it were worthless is indeed sheer intellectual imbecility. But for the wealth which has been gradually accumulated in this country, and which is sunk in its roads, its bridges, its canals, its railways, its harbours, its manufactories, its machinery, its tools, its steamships, its sailing-vessels; in the drainage and fencing of the land; in farm buildings and in stock; in the workings of its mines of coal and iron; in the millions of houses of brick and stone which have been built to be the homes of the people; in the water supply, the gas supply, and the sewers of its towns and cities,—but for the property which is held by Englishmen in a thousand industrial undertakings in other countries,—but for the circulating capital of the country,—but for all this wealth, our immense and constantly increasing population would have neither food to eat, nor clothes to wear, nor roofs to sleep under,—to say nothing of the total disappearance of all the resources and instruments of intellectual culture, and of all that contributes to the ease and refinement and delight of civilised life. To treat wealth—the wealth accumulated by the skill and industry and genius and thrift of many centuries—as though it were worthless, is to disregard the immense difference between barbarism and civilisation. Wealth has its place and value in the life of man. But it has so great a place that where the estimate of its worth is not controlled and corrected by Christian faith, it turns men aside—whether they are rich or poor—from their supreme duty and their supreme blessedness.

Rich men, who have an extravagant opinion of the worth of riches, become self-confident and arrogant; poor men, who have an extravagant opinion of the worth of riches, become the sycophants of the rich treat them with unmanly servility, or regard them with envy and jealousy. They become restless and discontented. The rich are sometimes insolent to the poor because of their poverty; the poor are sometimes insolent to the rich because of their riches. And all this is inconsistent with the spirit and temper of the Christian faith.

'*Hold not the faith of our Lord Jesus Christ, the Lord of Glory, with respect of persons.*' The rule for Jewish magistrates is the rule for Christian conduct: 'Ye shall do no unrighteousness in judgment: thou shalt not respect the person of the poor, nor honour the person of the mighty: but in righteousness shalt thou judge thy neighbour.'[1] To treat the rich unjustly because they are rich is a crime in a judge; to treat the poor unjustly because they are poor is also a crime in a judge. Insolence to the rich because they are rich—insolence to the poor because they are poor—the flattery of the rich because they are rich—the flattery of the poor because they are poor—are equally offences against the law of Christian justice, Christian courtesy, and Christian brotherhood. Strip off the mask, whether of wealth or of poverty, and judge men and treat men for what they are.

To show respect for age, for official position, for authority, respect for intellectual power and distinction, respect for character,—this is a Christian duty. For subjects to show respect to the sovereign, for

[1] Leviticus xix. 15.

citizens to show respect to municipal authorities, for soldiers to show respect to their officers, for workmen to show respect to their employers, who, as Mr. Carlyle called them, are 'captains of industry,'—this is a Christian duty: it is essential to the order and security and quiet working of the organisation of society. To show respect to a man who by his ability and industry and foresight and integrity has managed a great industrial undertaking successfully, has given regular employment through many years to hundreds of workmen, to whom he has paid fair wages, and whom he has treated with justice and generosity; to show respect, I say, to a man who has accumulated a great fortune by honourable means, and who uses his wealth for the public benefit as well as for personal enjoyment,—this is not unworthy of a man who has seen the glory of Christ.

We owe reverence to every man: for every man was created in the image of God, and shares the nature which was assumed by Christ, '*the Lord of Glory.*' Under all the distinctions which separate men from each other, the man who has Christian faith will recognise the greatness and the sacredness of human life. And yet while all share this greatness and this sacredness, there are real differences between men, and these too should be recognised. In the quaint, but stately words of Sir Thomas Browne: 'There is a Nobility without Heraldry, a natural dignity, whereby one man is ranked with another, another filed before him, according to the quality of his Desert, and pre-eminence of his good parts.'[1] This natural dignity may be wanting in a duke; it may be found in a peasant. Wherever it is found it should be reverenced. If found in the rich it should be honoured; if found in the poor it should be honoured. But to do honour to a man simply because he is rich, no matter how he got his wealth or how he spends it; to forgive him all his vices, to exaggerate all his virtues, because he is rich,—this is a crime. And if to this be added contempt for the poor, though their poverty may be dignified with uncomplaining patience, and faultless integrity, and unwearying industry,—the crime becomes still more flagrant.

James treats it as a grave and serious offence, it is an offence against '*the royal law, Thou shalt love thy neighbour*'—thy poor neighbour and thy rich neighbour alike—'*Thou shalt love thy neighbour as thyself.*' That is '*the royal law*,'—royal because it has the highest place among all the commandments prescribing our duties to other men, and royal, perhaps, because there is a certain kingly greatness in the spirit and character of the righteousness which it requires. For if we love our neighbour as ourselves, there is nothing servile in the discharge of our duties to him. We do him justice, not reluctantly and under the rigid constraint of an external law, but at the impulse of a free affection. Nor are we content to do him justice merely; our affection for

[1] Sir Thomas Browne's *Religio Medici*, part 2, § 1.

him leads us to do for him more than bare justice can demand, to render him services which no exact and legal estimate of his claims would require. There is nothing mean or niggardly in our treatment of him. We treat him with princely liberality. The law is a '*royal law*.'

James says that the law is transgressed if we have respect of persons. We do not love our neighbour as ourselves if we are discourteous to the poor; and it is an ignoble selfishness which leads us to treat the rich with servility and adulation. And although we keep the law in every other respect, if we commit these offences, we '*become guilty of all*.' He means that to break a law in any one of its requirements is to disregard and disobey the authority by which the whole law is given and sanctioned. If a man commits murder he transgresses the law, although he may be innocent of adultery, '*For he that said, Do not commit adultery, said also, Do not kill*.'

That is a principle which many of us fail to remember. We regard ourselves with complacency because we are free from the sins of which some of our neighbours are guilty, and we forget that if we are guilty of other sins we too are transgressors. A man thinks of himself with great satisfaction because he is temperate, industrious, thrifty. But he is guilty of the sin of selfishness and want of generosity. God who requires him to be temperate, industrious, and thrifty, also requires him to be unselfish and generous: he is a transgressor. A man is full of kindly impulses and is lavish in his generosity, but he is vain and ambitious. God who requires him to be kindly and generous, also requires him to be humble: he is a transgressor. A man is considerate to his social inferiors, but he is disrespectful and insolent in his language about men whose position is higher than his own. God requires him to be courteous to all men: he is a transgressor. A man is eager and earnest in good works for the relief of human suffering; but he neglects worship, there is no fervour in his prayers, he has no hearty gratitude for God's grace, no deep reverence for God's authority. The same law that requires him to love his neighbour as himself, requires him to love God with all his heart and soul and mind and strength: he is a transgressor. '*Whosoever shall keep the whole law, and yet stumble in one point, he is become guilty of all.*' Human life is surrounded by a hedge of divine commandments; one man breaks through it at one point, another at another. Wherever we break through, we are transgressors. There are a hundred ways in which we may show our want of reverence for God's authority; in whatever way we show it we are guilty of sin.

What then is the conclusion of the whole matter? '*So speak ye, and so do,*' says James, '*as men that are to be judged by a law of liberty.*' I have already endeavoured to explain what James means by that striking paradox—the law of liberty. The law which we have to obey—the law by which we shall be judged—is not a law which, like all human legislation, defines in precise terms the acts and the words which it forbids, or imposes a mere external restraint on speech and conduct. It is a law which demands and inspires the free consent of the heart. It is what has been called in the earlier part of this passage the '*royal law.*' It is less concerned with forbidding sins than with requiring the virtues which make the sins impossible. It is not satisfied with saying that we are not to bear false witness against men: it requires us to love them; and then we shall be slow to believe evil of others, and still slower to speak it. It is not satisfied with saying that we must not steal: it requires us to love men; and then instead of depriving them of their rights, we shall give them more than their due. It is not satisfied with saying that we are to do no harm to men: it requires us to love them; and then we shall dread to do them harm, and shall be eager to do them good.

This is the law by which we shall be judged, and James warns us that '*judgment is without mercy to him that hath showed no mercy.*' That we have not wronged men will not be enough to save us from condemnation in that last and awful day when we stand before God to give account of the deeds done in the body. Have we loved them? Have we been merciful to them? If we have, we shall be without fear; or if conscious of failure, and trembling in the presence of the majesty of God, His goodness will reassure us. At the very bar of the Eternal, those who have been filled with the spirit of love will have confidence and joy; or, in the vivid language of James, mercy glorieth even there—'*mercy glorieth against judgment.*' The teaching of James is the teaching of Paul: 'If I speak with the tongues of men and of angels, but have not love, I am become sounding brass, or a clanging cymbal. And if I have the gift of prophecy, and know all mysteries and all knowledge; and if I have all faith, so as to remove mountains, but have not love, I am nothing. And if I bestow all my goods to feed the poor, and if I give my body to be burned, but have not love, it profiteth me nothing. . . . Now abideth faith, hope, love'—these three are eternal—'and the greatest of these is Love.'[1]

[1] 1 Cor. xiii. 1-3, 13.

VI

FAITH AND WORKS

'*What doth it profit, my brethren, if a man say he hath faith, but have not works? can that faith save him? If a brother or sister be naked, and in lack of daily food, and one of you say unto them, Go in peace, be ye warmed and filled; and yet ye give them not the things needful to the body; what doth it profit? Even so faith, if it have not works, is dead in itself. Yea, a man will say, Thou hast faith, and I have works: shew me thy faith apart from thy works, and I by my works will shew thee my faith. Thou believest that God is one; thou doest well: the devils also believe, and shudder. But wilt thou know, O vain man, that faith apart from works is barren? Was not Abraham our father justified by works, in that he offered up Isaac his son upon the altar? Thou seest that faith wrought with his works, and by works was faith made perfect; and the scripture was fulfilled which saith, And Abraham believed God, and it was reckoned unto him for righteousness; and he was called the friend of God. Ye see that by works a man is justified, and not only by faith. And in like manner was not also Rahab the harlot justified by works, in that she received the messengers, and sent them out another way? For as the body apart from the spirit is dead, even so faith apart from works is dead.*'—JAMES ii. 14-26.

THIS vigorous and dramatic passage is so clear that it requires scarcely any explanation. James has been insisting earlier in the Epistle on the necessity of being '*doers of the word and not hearers only.*' He has said that '*whosoever shall keep the whole law, and yet stumble in one point, he is become guilty of all. For he that said, Do not commit adultery, said also, Do not kill. Now if thou dost not commit adultery, but killest, thou art become a transgressor of the law . . . judgment is without mercy to him that hath showed no mercy: mercy glorieth against judgment.*'

At this point he remembers that there are Jewish Christians who believed that they were certain to escape eternal death, and to have a place in the kingdom of God, because they held a true religious creed. It was one of the greatest and most powerful traditions of the Jewish race that they were separated from all the rest of mankind, not only by the great hopes which they inherited from Abraham, but by the belief that there is but one God, Creator of heaven and of earth, the Lord and Ruler of all nations. This belief, as they supposed, gave them great merit in the sight of God; and the merit of belief in the unity of God was extended to the belief in the other great articles of the Jewish creed; so that later Jewish doctors are quoted as maintaining that 'as soon as a man has mastered the thirteen heads of the faith, firmly believing therein, he is to be loved and forgiven and treated in all respects as a brother; and though he may have sinned in every possible way, he is indeed an erring Israelite, and is punished accordingly, but still he inherits eternal life.'[1] And there were Jewish Christians in the time of James who attached the same decisive value to their Christian faith. They were certain to resent the vehemence with which in the early part of this Epistle he insists

[1] Lightfoot, *Epistle to the Galatians*, p. 160.

on the necessity of good works. I can imagine them saying that he was treating those who believed that God is One, and that Jesus Christ was the true Lord and Saviour of men, as though they were no better than the miserable heathen who were worshipping countless gods of wood and stone. These men supposed that their faith would win for them the approval of God, whatever their works might be. James thinks it necessary to turn upon them, and he turns upon them with a fierceness which before he closes becomes terrific.

'*What doth it profit, my brethren, if a man say he hath faith, but have not works? can that faith save him?*' Some expositors have thrown the emphasis of the first question—on the word *say*; as though James had meant that for a man to *say* that he has faith, while the absence of good works proves that he has none, will not profit him. But the whole movement of thought in the following verses shows that this was not James's meaning. A man says he has faith, and yet it is apparent that he is not living a good life. James does not raise the question whether what the man says about his faith is true or not; he accepts the man's word: the man says he has faith, but he has not works; what James wants to know is whether that faith can profit him, can save him.

He sustains his question by an illustration. If a brother or sister is badly clothed, and ill-fed, and one of you say to them, '*Go in peace, be ye warmed and filled*'; but give them neither food nor clothing,—'*what doth it profit?*'

'*Be ye warmed and filled.*' These are no doubt very pleasant and very kindly words. If the man who utters them has given orders to his servants to get clothing for the poor people and to give them a good dinner, they are admirable. The words sound as if such orders had been actually given. But if the man sends away men and women in distress with words such as these, without doing anything to warm them or to fill them, '*what doth it profit?*' His compassion—if you will call it compassion—is a dead thing. And so a man's faith, if it have not works, profits nothing. You may call it faith, but it is dead. It is not merely without force to show itself in conduct; the faith itself is wholly without life; it '*is dead in itself.*' What can a dead faith do for a man?

Then James brings a third person into the discussion, and the third person shares in his own judgment on the controversy. The new-comer, assailing the man who thinks faith is enough without works, says in substance, You have faith—at least this is your claim; but I have to take your word for it. Show me your faith apart from your works; and I, on my part, by my works will show you my faith. How will you show your faith without works? That you have it, is not denied. But what proof can you give that you have it? I, on the other hand—so the third person in the little drama is represented as saying—'*I by my works will shew thee my faith.*'

There is another and a very vigorous thrust before the argument passes into a calmer mood. '*Thou believest that God is one.*' I will not deny the reality of thy faith, though thou hast no works by which to prove it. I accept thy statement. '*Thou believest that God is one; thou doest well.*' So far thou art wholly in the right; but dost thou imagine that this will save thee? '*The devils also believe*' that God is one, '*and they shudder.*' After that there is not very much to be said on behalf of the saving power of a true creed that does not lead to righteous living. A faith which is shared by devils cannot save a man.

I suppose that at this point the third person whom James has introduced into the discussion disappears, and James himself takes up the argument. Do you wish to know, he says, '*O vain man*'—empty, shallow, unreal man, taking words for things, mere forms for eternal realities,—do you wish to know, to have a decisive proof, '*that faith apart from works is barren*'? Look at Abraham, to whom you appeal as the great example and demonstration of the worth and power of faith. '*Was not Abraham our father justified by works, in that he offered up Isaac his son upon the altar? Thou seest that faith wrought with his works, and by works was faith made perfect; and the scripture was fulfilled which saith, And Abraham believed God, and it was reckoned unto him for righteousness: and he was called the friend of God. Ye see that by works a man is justified, and not only by faith.*' Take another example. When the spies that Joshua sent into Canaan to discover and report to him the condition of the country, and the strength of the inhabitants for resisting the invasion of Israel, came to Jericho, they were received by Rahab the harlot, and they lodged in her house. The king of Jericho discovered that strangers were in the city, and that Rahab had received them. But she told the king's messengers that her guests had left her about the time that the gates of the city were shut, and that she did not know where they were gone. The spies themselves she hid, and she gave us her reason for hiding them—'I know that the Lord hath given you the land, and that your terror is fallen upon us.' She spoke of the great deliverance which God had already wrought for Israel, and added, 'as soon as we had heard it, our hearts did melt . . . for the Lord your God, he is God in heaven above and on earth beneath.'[1] And she sent them off in a direction opposite to that which had been taken by their pursuers. The story was known to every Jew, and it was known that because of what Rahab had done she and her house were saved when Jericho was destroyed. And so James asks, '*Was not also Rahab the harlot justified by works, in that she received the messengers and sent them out another way?*'

Having given these two examples, James concludes his argument with the words, '*As the body apart from the spirit is dead, even so faith apart*

[1] Joshua ii. 1-14.

from works is dead'—a sentence which bears upon it the stamp of the originality and tendency to paradox characteristic of the mind of James. Faith is the inward and animating principle of righteousness. It gives life to works instead of receiving life from them; and this was the view of James himself. Faith, he has just said, apart from works, is barren, ineffective, fruitless. It is from faith that good works are to grow. And he has said again that when Abraham offered Isaac, '*faith wrought with his works, and by works was faith perfected.* Abraham's faith reached its end and consummation in Abraham's works, as the life of a tree reaches its end and consummation in the fruit. But here he changes the figure, and the change is striking and impressive. Faith he now regards as the body, but without works it is a dead body. Faith, he is ready to admit, gives to a man the outward and visible form of godliness. It is a body which may have beauty and the appearance of strength. But let us watch it: does it move? is there vigour in the hand and the foot? can they act? can they work? If not, the faith is dead. The life of the body is shown in action; the life of faith in good works.

About the meaning of this passage there can be no uncertainty. Every sentence is clear, intense, vivid. James maintains that faith apart from works is '*dead*,' '*barren*;' that such a faith cannot profit a man; that by works a man is justified, and not only by faith. The energy, not to say the vehemence, with which these statements are urged, shows that in the judgment of James he was insisting on one of the great truths of the Christian Gospel. The real difficulty arises from the fact that there are phrases in this passage which are so like some of the phrases in Paul's Epistles to the Galatians and the Romans, in which what appears to be quite a different position is maintained, that we can hardly resist the conclusion that James had read Paul's Epistles, if Paul wrote first, or that Paul had read James's Epistle, if James wrote first.

For example, James says, '*Faith apart from works is dead*,' '*is barren*.'[1] Paul says, 'We reckon therefore that a man is justified by faith apart from the works of the Law.'[2] James says, '*By works a man is justified, and not only by faith*.'[3] Paul says, 'A man is not justified by the works of the Law, save'—or, but only—'through faith in Jesus Christ.'[4] James appeals to Abraham, and maintains that '*Abraham our father*' was '*justified by works, in that he offered up Isaac his son upon the altar*.'[5] Paul appeals to Abraham, and maintains that 'if Abraham was justified by works he hath whereof to glory.'[6] But, he adds, It is impossible that he should have anything to glory in 'toward God.' 'For what saith the scripture? And Abraham believed God, and it was reckoned unto him for righteousness. Now to

[1] James ii. 17, 20.
[2] Rom. iii. 28.
[3] James ii. 24.
[4] Galatians ii. 16.
[5] James ii. 21.
[6] Rom. iv. 2-4.

him that worketh, the reward is not reckoned as of grace, but of debt.'[1]

I think that these passages make it evident that if Paul wrote first, James meant to correct Paul; and that if James wrote first, Paul meant to correct James. There are, I think, decisive reasons for believing that James wrote first;[2] and in that case it is probable that the passages in the Epistles to the Romans and the Galatians were intended by Paul to prevent a mischievous use of this passage in the Epistle of James.

There was, however, no real conflict between the position maintained by Paul and the position maintained by James. The difference between them does not relate to the substance of Christian truth. It was merely a difference in their method of stating it. James believed as strongly as Paul in the central and decisive importance of faith. To him, as well as to Paul, faith was the first and great demand of the Gospel of Christ, and the characteristic force of the Christian life. To him the trials by which a Christian man is tested and perfected are the proofs of his *faith*.[3] The condition on which God answers our prayer is that we 'ask *in faith*, nothing doubting.'[4] To be a Christian is to 'hold *the faith* of our Lord Jesus Christ,' and to hold this faith is inconsistent 'with respect of persons.'[5] In defending the poor from unkindly and inconsiderate treatment,

[1] Rom. iv. 3-4. [2] See *Mayor*, Introduction, pp. lxxxvii. foll.
[3] James i. 3. [4] James i. 6. [5] James ii. 1.

he asks, 'Did not God choose them that are poor as to the world to be rich *in faith*, and heirs of the kingdom which He promised to them that love Him?'[1] Even in this passage he is very far from setting works over against faith, as though works, not faith, were the condition of our salvation. Look at what he says about Abraham. He quotes the great words, 'Abraham believed God, and it was reckoned to him for righteousness;' and he says that when he offered Isaac his son upon the altar, Abraham's 'faith wrought with his works, and by works was faith made perfect.' If in any sense a man is justified by his works, it is because the works are the result of his faith, and in his works faith reaches the perfection of its power.

Again, the third person that James introduces into the controversy did not maintain that works apart from faith will save a man; he says, 'Show me thy faith apart from thy works, and I by my works will show thee my faith.'[2] Works which do not show faith, works which might be done apart from faith,—for these James has nothing to say.

And Paul insists as earnestly as James on the necessity of obedience to the will of God,—on the necessity of good works if we are to be saved. Writing to the Thessalonians,[3] he speaks of 'remembering without ceasing' their 'work of faith' as well as their 'labour of love.' Their faith was not barren or dead; it worked. Writing to the

[1] James ii. 5. [2] James ii. 18. [3] 1 Thess. i. 3.

Galatians,[1] he says that what avails for salvation is 'faith working through love.' In the Epistle to the Romans he repels with passion the charge that his teaching about justification by faith rendered good works unnecessary: 'Shall we continue in sin, that grace may abound? God forbid. We who died to sin, how shall we any longer live therein? . . . Let not sin therefore reign in your mortal body, that ye should obey the lusts thereof: neither present your members unto sin as instruments of unrighteousness; but present yourselves unto God, as alive from the dead, and your members as instruments of righteousness unto God. For sin shall not have dominion over you: for ye are not under law; but under grace.'[2]

James believed that in order to be saved we must have faith in Christ, but that the faith is unreal and worthless that does not show itself in works. Paul believed the same. But James stated the truth in a form which Paul thought likely to be perverted by the Judaisers who were corrupting the Gospel of Christ. James seems to have reasoned in this way: The Gospel of Christ requires men to have faith in Christ; but there may be a faith which seems to be real, and is yet unreal—a barren faith, a dead faith, and this is wholly worthless; a living faith will always show itself in good works. Apart from good works, therefore, a man is never justified; for apart from good works there is no living faith.

[1] Gal. v. 6. [2] Rom vi. 1, 2, 12-14.

There are men who are mistaking a dead faith for a living one, and are deluding themselves with the conviction that this faith will save them. The shortest, the sharpest, the most decisive method with such men is to insist that they are justified by the works in which faith is perfected.

James was a moralist, not a theologian. He is not speculative, but dramatic; he has as much of the Jewish prophet as of the Christian Apostle in him. He is eager for practice. When he sees men relying for salvation on a mere intellectual belief of the Christian Gospel, he will not stop to discuss whether their belief is of the right kind or not; he is certain that no belief will justify them which is not shown in good works; and the readiest way to force this home upon them was to insist that good works were necessary to their justification.

But although this may have been the most practical and effective method of dealing with the men whom James is assailing; although its rough, strong, and impressive statement of the truth may in their case have been more effectual for moral and spiritual purposes than a statement more concise and more accurate, Paul was not willing that phrases so easily misunderstood and so easily perverted should go without correction. The manner in which he deals with James's appeal to the example of Abraham is very striking. James asks, '*Was not Abraham our father justified by works, in that he offered up Isaac his son upon the altar? Thou seest that faith wrought with his works, and by works was faith made perfect; and the scripture was fulfilled which saith, And Abraham believed God, and it was reckoned unto him for righteousness.*'[1] Paul, in the Epistle to the Romans, points out that the great words, Abraham 'believed in the Lord, and He counted it to him for righteousness'[2] did not refer to the offering of Isaac, Abraham's most conspicuous act of obedience, but to Abraham's faith in God's promise that he should have a child, and that from that child there would spring an immense number of descendants.[3] 'The Lord came unto Abraham in a vision, saying, Fear not, Abraham, I am thy Shield, and thy exceeding great Reward.' Abraham answered despondingly that however good God might be to himself, he had no children to inherit God's blessing. Isaac was not yet born; Ishmael was not yet born; his steward, Eliezer of Damascus, was his heir. God answered him that his heir would be not Eliezer, but a child of his own; and the story goes on: 'He brought him forth abroad, and said, Look now toward heaven, and tell the stars, if thou be able to tell them: and He said unto him, So shall thy seed be. And he believed in the Lord; and He counted it to him for righteousness.'[4] It was not because in the power of faith he obeyed God by offering Isaac upon the altar that his faith was reckoned for righteousness, but because he believed

[1] James ii. 21-23.
[2] Genesis xv. 6.
[3] Romans iv. 16-22.
[4] Genesis xv. 1-6.

the divine promise that his descendants were to be countless as the stars.

James, indeed, does not say that the offering of Isaac was reckoned to Abraham for righteousness ; he says that in the offering of Isaac the scripture which saith, Abraham 'believed God, and it was reckoned unto him for righteousness,' was fulfilled. By this I suppose he meant that the scripture declared that Abraham's belief in the divine promise of a son was imputed to him for righteousness, and that the declaration would surely hold true, would be 'fulfilled,' when Abraham's faith rose to such energy as to make him ready to offer his son in obedience to the divine command. What was true of the earlier and less vigorous faith—that it was imputed to Abraham for righteousness—must, if possible, have been still more true of that later and more energetic faith which was expressed in the offering of Isaac. It was the faith that was reckoned—not the work.

But Paul saw that to connect the offering of Isaac with the reckoning of his faith to Abraham for righteousness was likely to be misunderstood; and therefore in the Epistle to the Romans he recalls the original story. It was Abraham's belief in the promise that he should be the head of a great race, not the offering of Isaac, which, according to the Scriptures, was reckoned to him for righteousness.

It was Paul's great commission to make clear to the Church of all ages the absolute freedom of the grace of God. It was for him to show, with incomparable power, that every blessing that God confers upon us is a free gift, and is not in any sense or in any degree a reward that we deserve by our righteousness. Whatever righteousness we may achieve constitutes no claim on our part upon God. The measure of our righteousness is also the measure of our debt to Him; for if we are righteous, we are righteous in God's strength, not in our own:—

'All that I was, my sin, my guilt,
My death, was all my own:
All that I am I owe to Thee,
My gracious Lord, alone.'

And yet Paul insisted on the necessity of good works and on the awfulness of Judgment to come.

He would have gone heart and soul with the real drift of the vigorous appeal of James in this passage, though he was dissatisfied with some of its phrases. He, too, would have said, '*Shew me thy faith, apart from thy works, and I by my works will shew thee my faith.*' I think I see these two great teachers of the Church standing among us this morning and appealing to man after man in this congregation. It matters not which of them speaks,—Paul or James; both of them would ask you to show your faith by your works, and would tell you that the faith is dead and barren that is apart from works.

The works they would demand are works which show faith; these, and these alone, would satisfy them. You are honest—yes, and so are multitudes of men who have no faith. You are truthful—yes, and so are multitudes of men who have no faith: kindly, generous, temperate—yes, and so are multitudes of men who have no faith. Honesty, truthfulness, kindliness, generosity, temperance,—all these must be present in your life and conduct, or you are no Christian. But you may have all these virtues and not be a Christian: you may find them in the lives of heathen men and of atheists; they can therefore be no proofs of faith. You read the Bible, you offer private prayer, you attend worship regularly, you contribute, perhaps liberally, towards great religious objects. Yes,—but you know very well that men do all these things and yet show by their conduct that they have no real faith. These things therefore cannot be relied upon as proofs that you have faith.

'*Shew me thy faith by thy works.*' You believe that God in His infinite love sent the Lord Jesus Christ to be the Saviour of men: what proof is there in your life of the reality of your belief? Does the wonder which this immense manifestation of the love of God should create, or the gratitude, or the joy, show itself in your spirit and conduct? You believe that Christ is the Lord of Life: what do you do that you would not do if you did not believe it? You believe that Christ came to save all men: what effect does that faith have upon your actions? What sympathy do you show with Christ's great purpose? What are you doing that men may know what Christ has done and endured for them? You believe in Judgment to come: do you? From what sin does it restrain you? To what duty that would be otherwise neglected does it impel you? Have you avoided a single sinful habit or a single sinful act through dread of that final account? You believe that God is your Father: do you? Be honest with yourself, and ask what difference it would make,—not in the sentiment of life, but in your actual conduct,—if you ceased to believe it. Your children, I suppose, could tell you of a dozen things they did or left undone last week because they respect your authority. How many things have you done, or left undone, last week because you respect God's authority? You believe that there is a heaven on the other side of death: do you? Does your belief make any difference to you? Does it make you more patient in trouble? Does it keep your heart quiet when you suffer injustice? Does it enable you to bear losses with less agitation? Does it lead you to place an altogether different estimate on wealth, and all that wealth can purchase, from that which other men place who do not believe in heaven? Does it make you less eager for social position and public honour? Are you doing anything to make your place in heaven sure beyond all doubt? Does the bare possibility of missing heaven fill you with dismay and distress? Paul, James—either of them—might ask these questions. I entreat every one of you to endeavour to answer them honestly, and to remember that if a man say he hath faith and have not works—works which are the clear result of his faith—that faith cannot save him.

VII

THE PERILS OF SPEECH

'*Be not many teachers, my brethren, knowing that we shall receive heavier judgment. For in many things we all stumble. If any stumbleth not in word, the same is a perfect man, able to bridle the whole body also. Now if we put the horses' bridles into their mouths, that they may obey us, we turn about their whole body also. Behold the ships also, though they are so great, and are driven by rough winds, are yet turned about by a very small rudder, whither the impulse of the steersman willeth. So the tongue also is a little member, and boasteth great things. Behold, how much wood is kindled by how small a fire! And the tongue is a fire: the world of iniquity among our members is the tongue, which defileth the whole body, and setteth on fire the wheel of nature, and is set on fire by hell.*'—JAMES iii. 1-6.

'*BE not many teachers, my brethren, knowing that we shall receive heavier judgment.*'—These words remind us of the large freedom of speech which existed in the early Christian Church. The ordinary Church assemblies in the first age were very like the Church Conferences which we often hold during the winter months. Every Church had its official rulers or leaders; in Churches consisting chiefly of Jews, they were called elders; in Churches consisting chiefly of Christian Gentiles, they were called bishops. Each at first had several elders, several bishops. When the Church met for worship, fellowship, or instruction, an elder or a bishop presided; but prayers were offered and hymns were sung by private members of the Church, and private members were also at liberty to instruct the Church in Christian truth, to exhort it to the discharge of Christian duty, and to dwell on the great hopes of the Church, and on the blessedness which had come to it through Christ.

It is very clear from Paul's Epistles to the Corinthians that at Corinth some men who had real spiritual gifts used them for the purpose of personal vanity, and thought more of the admiration which they might excite by the display of their powers, than of the light and strength which through God's grace they might give to their brethren. It is also clear that others were contentious and endeavoured to draw to themselves a party in the Church. And these words of James's, in which he warns the Jewish Christians against being anxious to become teachers, show that in the Jewish Churches much of the speaking was inconsiderate, reckless, and not likely to contribute to edification.

He tells them that those who become teachers of the Church assume grave responsibilities. If through God's grace their teaching is true and wholesome, and contributes to the righteousness and power and joy of the Church, they will no doubt receive from God at last a nobler reward than if they were silent. But if not, they will receive heavier judgment. That makes the Christian ministry in our own times a perilous as well as a glorious service. If through the light and power of the Spirit of God I am able, week after week, to make clearer to you the righteousness and the grace and the glory of God; if I am able to give you a truer and deeper knowledge of the Christian redemption; if while you listen to me, the laws of Christian duty become more definite and more authoritative, and you receive strength to obey them more perfectly in your common life,—then, O blessed thought! my ministry will be approved of God in that Great Day. But, if through carelessness, through haste, through intellectual and moral presumption,—if through my personal sinfulness, which must obscure my vision of God and corrupt my conception of Christian conduct, —if through a defective spiritual experience, through want of prayer, and an unwillingness to wait humbly and reverently for the illumination of the Holy Spirit,—if through reluctance to dwell on truths and duties by which my own unfaithfulness is rebuked, or which I know would provoke, if I preached them, your resentment and antagonism,—if, I say, through any of these causes I myself fail to reach the very truth of God, and fail to make it known, my condemnation at the last will be severer and more terrible than yours. I may be saved—saved through the grace of God from utter ruin and from eternal death—but I shall be saved like a man who is dragged out of a burning house; he is alive, but the fierce fire has scorched him, and he has lost everything but life.

And the same heavier judgment will come upon all teachers of the Church who are guilty of similar sins. I assume that no Christian man will teach what he knows to be false; his real peril lies in the failure to be devout, serious, patient in discovering the truth. The danger does not threaten the ministry only. It threatens all who undertake to form the opinions of other men on Christian truth and Christian hope and Christian duty.

I received only last week a letter from an unknown correspondent, living at a distance, which may illustrate the danger. The writer said: 'I am the leader of a Men's Bible Class, which consists of about thirty members. They are anxious for me to speak on Eternal Punishment. . . . I am only a young man among them, and have really no definite belief upon the subject. I am at present wavering between the total annihilation of the wicked, as appears to be indicated in so many places, or universalism—the latter seeming the most rational. If it is not asking too much, I should esteem it a great favour if you could just counsel me which way to turn, and what course to pursue in respect to the subject.' I hardly knew what my correspondent expected me to answer him. He might perhaps—I could not tell—he might perhaps have expected me to write him a letter explaining my own position and the ground of it; or he might have thought that I should recommend him some little book which he could read through in an hour, and so form his judgment. For I nearly always find that correspondents of this description imagine that what they can read in an hour ought to be enough to enable them to form a final judgment on the greatest questions which perplex human thought. But if I had taken either of these courses, I should have done my part to make him unfaithful to God and to man. The subject is an awful one. The judgment we form, as between the two conceptions which appeared to divide the mind of my correspondent, must have the gravest effect on our own spiritual life, and the gravest effect on the lives of those whom we persuade to accept our judgment. Are all men, whatever their lives in this world, to dwell in God's glory for ever? Or is it possible that some—that many—may through persistent indifference to God's authority and to the grace of Christ, miss that glory? Our decision between these alternatives must make an infinite difference to us and to other men whose judgment we may influence. It is of the gravest consequence that we should discover, if we can, which alternative is true.

I recommended my unknown friend to tell his class what a fearful responsibility it was for any man to form and to express a judgment on the question; to tell them that, as yet, to use his own words, he had 'no definite belief' about it, and that he did not dare to speak to them until he had. I further recommended him to read the New Testament through very carefully, that he might learn what

Christ and His Apostles taught on this subject, to pray to God to enable him to discover and to accept what they taught. If after reading through the New Testament he was not quite clear about his conclusions, I suggested that he should read two books on the subject, one on the side of Universalism, and the other on the side of what is known as the doctrine of Life in Christ, and then putting the books aside, read the New Testament through again, still praying to God to enable him to see what was the thought of Christ on this great subject. If at last he reached a definite conclusion, I advised him to be silent for a year before he attempted to draw others to the same judgment. I am glad to say that I received an answer from him promising to follow this advice.

You may say that this would discourage all religious teaching and all speech about religious truth. But no; there is a guilty silence as well as guilty speech. Some things a Christian man may know for himself with perfect assurance—the righteousness of God and His grace, the reality of the redemption achieved by Christ, the authority of Christ over conduct, the blessedness of restoration to God through Him; and of these we are under an obligation to speak. It is by our speaking of these that others are to be drawn out of darkness into the light of God; we are silent on them at our peril. But when we touch realms of uncertainty, let us hold our tongue, or at least cease to speak confidently.

It is on great questions of religious truth and duty that a man is bound to take the greatest pains before he reaches a conclusion and endeavours to propagate it. But it is also a duty to take pains in the formation of opinion on all other subjects of importance before we express judgments about them.

The habit of reckless talking about the character and doings of other people, about the capacity and the motives of public men, should be severely checked. It often inflicts the most cruel injustice. Nor should we be less careful in expressing our judgments on large subjects relating to the economic, social, and political life of the community. In a country like this, where public opinion affects legislation and government, every man who talks confidently on questions of this kind incurs grave responsibility. Ask yourselves, not what you have heard, but what you really know about the questions on which you speak. There are people who, on the strength of reading a halfpenny newspaper every evening, are able to criticise with an air of omniscience the policy of the most eminent statesmen belonging to both the great political parties. There are people who after listening to a few speeches and reading a few paragraphs on some great economic question, like bimetalism or the limitation of the hours of adult labour, assume that they can speak with contempt about some of the ablest men in England who have thought on these subjects for years, have read everything that has been written about them by eminent economists in this country, in France, Germany, Italy, and America, and have discussed them with men of their own intellectual rank. For most of us it is not possible to form an independent judgment that is worth anything on complicated subjects of this kind, and we should speak modestly about them if we speak at all. If we are compelled, as we often are, to support at the polling-booth one side or the other, we can only lean on the judgment of those who seem to us to be the most capable and the most upright men. But we should be careful in the choice of our authorities. If we are ill, we go to a doctor, not to a lawyer, though the lawyer may happen to be the more brilliant man. If we want to build a house, we go to an architect, not to a bricklayer. If we want to know the truth on some great scientific question, we ask what is the general judgment of the most eminent men in that department of science. If we want to know the truth on some question which can be settled only by scholars, we ask whether the most eminent scholars have reached any certain conclusion about it. On all questions of grave practical importance to the community, about which we cannot form an opinion of our own, we have, I say, to lean on the judgment of men who seem worthy of confidence—able men, men who have given their time and strength to subjects of this order, and whose spirit and sympathies seem to us just and generous. Having discovered their position and some of the grounds on which it rests, we may feel at liberty to defend and to advocate it; but we should remember that we ourselves are not authorities on the subject, and should not speak arrogantly, or with unmeasured assurance that we are in the right and that every one who differs from us is in the wrong.

The ordinary reply to cautions of this kind would be that all that is necessary to settle these questions is a little common sense,—and common sense is what every man thinks that he himself possesses, though it is very clear to him that a great many other people are destitute of it. But, as Archbishop Whately somewhere says, though men imagine that common sense is all that is necessary in order to deal with questions of which they know nothing, no man supposes that mere common sense is sufficient to deal with matters of which he himself has experience and knowledge. Large numbers of people, I suppose, think that common sense would be enough to settle nearly all the legal questions which are submitted to the Courts; no lawyer thinks so. Large numbers of people imagine that all that is necessary for a man to keep himself in health, and to deal with ordinary diseases, is a little common sense; no doctor thinks so. Manufacturers and shopkeepers, who have never been on the Town Council, or on the School Board, or on the Board of Guardians, imagine that a little common sense is all that is necessary to manage the affairs of the city, to conduct the schools, to relieve the poor. But if a man thought that a little common sense, without experience, was enough to enable a man to manage a brass manufactory, or a draper's shop, they would call him a fool. To settle questions, and to talk about questions, of which we know nothing, men think that we only need common sense; but as soon as we begin to know, we discover that knowledge and experience are necessary.

The great cause of danger in speaking, as James implies throughout this passage, is that vast numbers of people wholly fail to recognise how great a place our words must hold in our moral life, and how difficult it is always to speak truthfully, justly, and generously. The tongue is a little member, and we think that words are unimportant. '*In many things,*' James says, '*we all stumble.*' James did not imagine that either he himself or the Christian people about him had wholly escaped from sin. '*If any stumbleth not in word, the same is a perfect man, able to bridle the whole body also.*' Whoever, that is, has so much moral seriousness, so much vigilance, so much firmness, that he can keep his tongue under the control of God's laws, is a Christian of mature vigour—full grown; and he will have a complete moral mastery of himself.

The bridle that is put into the mouth of a horse is a very small thing compared with the horse; but if you have a firm hold of the bridle, you can turn his whole body as you please. The rudder is a very small thing compared with a great ship; but if you control the rudder, you can direct the ship's course.

'*So the tongue also is a little member, and boasteth great things.*' And James does not mean that there is no ground for its boasting. Small as it is, it can do great things—great good, or great mischief; and it is very hard to control.

'*Behold, how much wood*' (or, *how great a forest*) '*is kindled by how small a fire! And the tongue is a fire.*' Speech is a fire that can kindle into flame a whole forest, or, as he might have said, can cause the destruction of whole cities.

'*The world of iniquity among our members is the tongue*':—that is a very striking expression. James means, I think, that the sins which can be committed by every other member of the body—by the hand, or by the eye, for example—are limited and definite. The hand can strike a cruel and murderous blow; the eye can be the instrument of lust; but the tongue is the whole '*world of iniquity.*' There is no divine law that it cannot break. It may be guilty of irreverence to God and of profanity. It may be insolent to parents; it may be arrogant to all men. Not by the hand only can a man steal—he can rob his neighbour by lying words. Not by the hand only can he do violence to other men—by his tongue he can inflict the most cruel and intolerable suffering. His tongue may be the instrument of his hatred and of his lust. There is no sinful passion which may not find expression in speech, and by speech inflict deadly injury on the innocent and the just. There is no ambitious and selfish motive which may not achieve its ends by speech. The tongue is '*the world of iniquity among our members*': in speech every possible form of evil may have its place. And as in an earlier passage in this Epistle James tells us that true religion will lead a man to keep himself unspotted from the great world outside, which is likely to defile him, he here implies that true religion will lead a man to avoid defilement from that world of iniquity which he may find in his own speech.

Then he returns to the comparison of the tongue to a fire. He says that it '*setteth on fire the wheel of nature*,'—by which I suppose he means the course of human life,—'*and is set on fire by hell.*'

And is not this true? In families, among friends, what fires of evil passion are kindled by careless, reckless, and unkind speech! In churches, what fires of dissension are kindled by wilful, wayward, unconsidered, suspicious, ungenerous speech! In the community, what fierce disputes; what ruinous conflicts between different classes of men, who ought to work together for their own good and the good of the State, are provoked by ignorant and malignant speech! Wild, passionate words may kindle a whole nation into fierce hostility against its neighbours and rivals, and the flames may have to be quenched in blood. Yes, it is the very fire of hell that burns on the human tongue; and every Christian man should seek grace to extinguish the fire before it kindles the passions of other men.

VIII

THE DISCIPLINE OF THE TONGUE

'*For every kind of beasts and birds, of creeping things and things in the sea, is tamed, and hath been tamed by mankind: but the tongue can no man tame; it is a restless evil, it is full of deadly poison. Therewith bless we the Lord and Father; and therewith curse we men, which are made after the likeness of God: out of the same mouth cometh forth blessing and cursing. My brethren, these things ought not so to be. Doth the fountain send forth from the same opening sweet water and bitter? can a fig tree, my brethren, yield olives, or a vine figs? neither can salt water yield sweet.*'—JAMES iii. 7-12.

THERE is a striking contrast between the moral precepts of this Epistle and the moral precepts contained in most of the Epistles of Paul. Paul wrote to Churches in which there were large numbers of men and women who had been born heathen, and had lived a heathen life till manhood and womanhood. The stain of the grosser vices of heathenism had not wholly disappeared from their character. Their conscience was not severe in its condemnation of even very gross vices. And so Paul had to speak to them in plain language about coarse and disgraceful sins. James is writing to Christians who were born Jews, and who, before they became Christians, had been disciplined by the traditions and customs of Judaism. They, too, had their sins; but their sins were not of the sensual kind, against which Paul had to warn his converts from heathenism. Their own conscience condemned gross sensual vices, and they had been trained to avoid them.

What the law of Moses and the traditions of the Jewish race had done for Jewish Christians, the large influence which the Christian Church has exerted on the whole social and moral life of this country has done for us. The foul vices which Paul denounces in his letters to the Ephesians, the Thessalonians, the Corinthians, are not the vices into which those of us who were brought up among decent people in this country, even though they were not religious, are likely to be betrayed. It is in this letter, written by James to Christian Jews, that we shall find the moral precepts which we are most likely to transgress.

The lusts which James condemns are not the grosser lusts of the flesh, but the lusts which lead to envy, jealousy, and strife. The adultery which he denounces is an unlawful living with the world—unfaithfulness to God. Pride, selfishness, the love of money, reverence for rich men because they are rich, instability in God's service, want of kindliness, want of generosity, want of humility, reliance on the mere knowledge of what is true and right in the absence of a faithful discharge of quiet Christian duty,—these are among the things on which James pours out volcanic streams of condemnation. And these are the sins of which we ourselves are most likely to be guilty.

But there is one class of sins to which he returns again and again, his heat growing intenser whenever he returns to them. Sins of the tongue seem to have been so common among the Jewish Christians that James assails them in passage after passage, and assails them in language which is not only stern but fierce. In the very first chapter he entreats the Christian people to whom he is writing to be '*swift to hear, slow to speak*'; tells them that '*if any man thinketh himself to be religious, while he bridleth not his tongue,*' he is deceiving his own heart, and that '*this man's religion is vain.*' In the next chapter, he charges them not only to act, but to '*speak as men that are to be judged by a law of liberty.*' Christ has given them liberty, no doubt; but He will punish lawlessness whether in speech or in action; the liberty He gives is a liberty to fulfil the law, not to break it.

The passage about justification in which he insists that works are necessary to the justified man, as well as faith, was suggested no doubt by the number of great religious talkers in the Christian Jewish Churches; men who were always speaking about the soundness of their faith, but who were careless about practical Christian living. This third chapter is almost entirely occupied with sins of the tongue. In the middle of the fourth chapter he says, '*Speak not one against another, brethren. He that speaketh against a brother, or judgeth his brother, speaketh against the law, and judgeth the law'*—sets himself up as a judge; that is, overrides the law, and condemns the law, which reserves the judgment on every man to God. In the latter part of the same chapter he censures presumptuous and vaunting speech. In the fifth he condemns murmuring against other men, and swearing. A great part of the Epistle is written against sins of the tongue. That is very remarkable. It shows how liable men are to commit these sins; what guilt they incur, what harm they do, by committing them; and how hard it is to avoid them.

But how wonderful a faculty speech is! It makes human society possible. Apart from words—visible or audible signs expressing inward thought and feeling—the inner life of every man would be an island surrounded by an impassable ocean. There could be no commerce, no politics, no church. One great school of philosophy has maintained that apart from language—definite signs for ideas—there could even be no thought. How wonderful again, I say, is this faculty of speech! The words of a mother to her child, of a child to a mother—the words of lovers—the words of friends—the words of dying men—how these remain in the memory of those to whom they were spoken, a light, a joy, a power, through all succeeding years. What palaces of beauty the poets have built for us with words! What treasures of wisdom the wise of all countries and of all ages have laid up for us in words! The words of great political orators have changed the temper and the thoughts of nations, have provoked war, have compelled peace. The words of great preachers have shaken the hearts of men with fear, inspired them with immortal hope, made real the invisible and eternal kingdom of God. The words of prophets, of apostles, have wrought miracles in the moral life of men, in many centuries, in many lands. The words of Christ!—the accent of God is in them, and we listen with wonder and awe and immeasurable joy. And to describe the eternal glory of Christ Himself, we speak of Him as the *Word* of God.

Yes—speech is capable of great and noble uses. But it is also capable of uses most base, most malignant, and most foul. And James warns us that to govern the tongue, to restrain it from great and flagrant sins, is a task beyond human strength. Not to stumble in word, he has told us in the early part of the chapter, is the mark of a strong mature Christian life; and now he says that '*every kind of beasts and birds, of creeping things and things in the sea, is tamed and hath been tamed by mankind.*' There is that in the nature of man which can master and subdue the wildest and fiercest of the inferior races; '*but the tongue can no man tame.*' A diviner power than any which belongs to human nature apart from God is necessary for this task.

'*It is a restless evil*':—the evil is always active, and it assumes forms which are constantly changing; there is unjust and reckless censure of men one hour, and the next hour pernicious flattery; to-day a base apology and tenderness for bad men, which calls itself charity; to-morrow an ungenerous criticism of good men, which calls itself impartiality and justice; there is insolence, which calls itself independence; and this is followed by words of unmanly servility. '*The tongue is a restless evil.*'

'*It is full of deadly poison.*' James was thinking of the words of the Psalmist—'adders' poison is under their lips.'[1] There may be poison—'*deadly poison*'—in words. They may destroy purity; they may destroy faith in God; they may destroy trust in men; they may destroy the mutual affection of friends; they may destroy the peace of families; they may destroy the very life of Churches. Even apart from the deliberate intention to inflict these enormous injuries, careless words may inflict them. Words spoken in confidence are repeated, and repeated apart from other words which qualified their meaning, and apart from the circumstances which suggested them. Facts are inaccurately reported; motives are gratuitously imputed; men speak with imperfect knowledge of what other men have done,—tell half the truth, infer the rest; and their words become a '*deadly poison.*' They repeat what they have heard, when there was no occasion to repeat it; they think that it is a sufficient justification for what they tell one man, that other men have told them: they might as well plead that because some one has

[1] Psalm cxl. 3.

put into their hands a bottle of prussic acid, they are blameless for passing it on to a man who took it and died of it. They say that they have heard some evil report of a neighbour, but that they do not believe it. But the report creates suspicion, and the suspicion grows, and a man's reputation is murdered. If they did not believe the report, why did they pass it on? They see something which seems to them suspicious in another man's conduct; they ask him for no explanation, but they express their suspicion: their words are '*deadly poison*,' a friendship is ruined for ever.

It is not only for the words that are deliberately false that we shall have to give account, but for the words that are false through our haste, through our want of consideration, through our want of generous confidence in other men. It is not only for the words that are malignant that we shall have to give account, but for words spoken in carelessness and thoughtlessness, which had all the effect of words spoken malignantly.

James, in his vivid manner, then goes on to brand the abnormal, the monstrous nature of the sins of the tongue. '*Therewith bless we the Lord and Father; and therewith curse we men, which are made after the likeness of God: out of the same mouth cometh forth blessing and cursing. My brethren, these things ought not so to be. Doth the fountain send forth from the same opening sweet water and bitter? can a fig tree, my brethren, yield olives, or a vine figs? neither can salt water yield sweet.'* He means that if we have a real reverence and love for God, it will be impossible for us to utter bitter and cruel words about men. It is as impossible—this is James's contention—that a man who really blesses and praises God, should curse men, as that sweet water and salt water should come from the same spring.

I think that most of us must feel that James had a far graver sense of the moral and religious importance of words than is common even among Christian people. For him, words are deeds; they are decisive tests of the real quality of life. He had laid to heart the solemn declaration of our Lord, 'that every idle word that men shall speak, they shall give account thereof in the day of judgment. For by thy words' —not by thy actions alone—'by thy words thou shalt be justified, and by thy words thou shalt be condemned.'[1]

And I suppose that if we are to discipline the tongue, we must first of all endeavour to make real to ourselves the seriousness of speech. We should think about it day after day, until by God's grace we feel as we have never felt before, that our words are really a very large part of our moral life. For example, we should think of the suffering which has been inflicted on ourselves by careless or bitter words, of the injury which we know that such words have done to other men; we should think of the words which have rankled in our hearts for months or

[1] Matt. xii. 36, 37.

years—words which perhaps were never meant very seriously, and which we ought to have forgotten, but which have inflicted on us great misery, and alienated our hearts from brothers or sisters or friends. We should think of words which have stung us to passion; of words which have filled our imagination with foul shapes, that haunted us day after day, and refused to be banished; of words which have shaken our faith in God, and destroyed our comfort in His love. We should think of words which have created unjust suspicion of the integrity or the sobriety of other men, and have led to the loss of the confidence of their employers and to the ruin of their families. We should think of the wretched whisperers who have quenched the love of wives for their husbands, and of husbands for their wives. We should think of how we ourselves have been misled, and involved in serious trouble, by the careless inaccuracy of the words of men whom we trusted. In every way that we can we should try to bring home to ourselves the truth, that words which are lightly spoken may be a grave offence against justice and against charity.

We should further consider, and consider seriously, the great warning of our Lord that for every 'idle word' that men shall speak they shall give account in the day of judgment. 'Idle words' are words which are spoken carelessly, indolently, without any moral effort to avoid sin: if they are sinful, our moral insensibility to their sinfulness will be no excuse for them. These are the words against which Christian people have to watch most carefully. When challenged about them, they say they never thought that what they said would do any harm; but it was because they never thought that their words were 'idle words.' They say that they never meant any harm, but they did harm; and if they had considered what they were saying, they would never have said it. And if for 'idle words' we must give account in the day of judgment—and Christ Himself, who warns us, will be the Judge—much more shall we give account of words which are not idle, careless, thoughtless; but which are deliberately false, uncharitable, and revengeful. We must give account; and even if, through God's grace, we are not shut out of the City of God, false words, uncharitable words, revengeful words, idle words, that pained and wronged other men, will impoverish our eternal reward, and lessen our eternal joy. Judgment to come should teach us to put a restraint on our speech.

And the striking words, '*Therewith bless we the Lord and Father, and therewith curse we men, which are made after the likeness of God*,' may also check rough, reckless, false, unkindly speech. Made 'in the image of God'[1]—that is true of all men; of those whose vices, or whose perversities, or whose weaknesses irritate us, anger us, provoke our scorn. With what courtesy born of religious reverence, with what scrupulous consideration, governed by the

[1] Gen. i. 27.

remembrance of the traces of the divine image—not yet wholly lost—should we treat all men, if we remembered the words of James. How shall we dare to give needless pain to men who are made in the likeness of God? For God's sake we shall be kindly to them. How shall we dare to speak of them unjustly? God will judge us, and they were made in the likeness of God. How shall we dare to speak to them insolently, or contemptuously? They were made in the likeness of God, and some day we may see them among the shining hosts of the Eternal City. With our tongue we have blessed God in the morning for His mercy to ourselves: how shall we dare during the day to speak unmercifully of men who were made in the likeness of God? We have entreated God to forgive us: how shall we dare to speak words on fire with revenge to those who are made in the likeness of God? Let our prayers and our thanksgivings check and control our common speech, and we may approach James's conception of the '*perfect man*,' who, stumbling not in word, '*is able to bridle the whole body also.*'

IX

THE WISDOM FROM ABOVE

'*Who is wise and understanding among you? let him shew by his good life his works in meekness of wisdom. But if ye have bitter jealousy and faction in your heart, glory not and lie not against the truth. This wisdom is not a wisdom that cometh down from above, but is earthly, sensual, devilish. For where jealousy and faction are, there is confusion and every vile deed. But the wisdom that is from above is first pure, then peaceable, gentle, easy to be entreated, full of mercy and good fruits, without variance, without hypocrisy. And the fruit of righteousness is sown in peace for them that make peace.*'—JAMES iii. 13-18.

JAMES is still thinking of the men whom he had assailed with such vigour in the first part of this chapter and the latter part of the preceding chapter —men who attached an inordinate value to what they supposed to be their true faith, but who in their spirit and conduct were gravely at fault—men who supposed that they had a deeper wisdom and a larger knowledge than their brethren, and who were continually asserting their claim to be teachers of the Church. He insists that where there is wisdom and understanding they are to be shown, not in mere words, but in a good life. The really wise man will not be guilty of self-assertion and arrogance. He will be gentle, modest, humble; his whole conduct will be distinguished by meekness of wisdom. If, on the other hand, James continues, any of you, because you imagine that you are wise, are bitterly jealous of the influence and authority of other men, whose claims to consideration, as you think, are inferior to your own; if you have a factious spirit, and endeavour to make a party in the Church in order that you may secure the ascendency of your own opinion and the success of your own schemes, '*glory not.*' That is, do not boast of your wisdom, do not regard yourself with self-complacency on account of it: if you do, you are lying against the truth; you are regarding as a divine gift what is an unspiritual and even devilish thing. This wisdom—a wisdom which leads men to bitter jealousy of their brethren, and to the creating of dissensions and factions in the Church—does not come down '*from above,*' '*but is earthly, sensual, devilish.*' For, he adds, '*where jealousy and faction are,*' there is no peace, no order, but '*confusion and every vile deed.*'

This is a dreary and depressing passage. It reminds us that the joy and strength of the Churches of Apostolic times were impaired by the very spirit and temper which have desolated the religious life of so many Churches in later generations. Even in those early days, there were men who had a measureless self-conceit, a bitter jealousy of those whom their brethren regarded with affection and trust, an arrogant confidence in their own opinion and their own judgment; men in whom there was very little of the spirit of Christ, but who were quite-certain that they, and they alone, had the mind of Christ; men who were resolved, whatever might come of it, to force upon the Church their own beliefs, either with regard to doctrine or practice; who made parties in the Church to carry out their purposes, held secret meetings, flattered those who stood by them as being faithful to conscience and to Christ, and disparaged the fidelity of all who differed from them. Even then such men broke up the peace of Churches, and in the confusion which they created many wicked things were said, and many wicked things were done. These men had power, real power of a kind; but it was not a wisdom that came '*from above*.' They showed the same kind of faculty that is possessed by men whose ambition is wholly earthly and unspiritual; they practised the same arts. Their power was a real power; but it was '*earthly, sensual, devilish.*' The passage stands on the pages of this Epistle as an awful warning to the Church of every generation.

Then follows the noble and beautiful account of the true wisdom—'*the wisdom that cometh down from above*'; and it will be well for us to consider one by one, and very carefully, its several characteristics.

As we have already seen, wisdom—in the sense in which it is used by James, and indeed in the Scriptures generally—is something wholly distinguishable from mere knowledge A man who has spent his entire life in mastering many provinces of learning, or who is familiar with some of the great realms of science, may have no wisdom, and a peasant who can barely read may be a wise man. The wise man has discovered the actual truth about the world and the order of human life. He has seen, and he never forgets, God's invisible and eternal kingdom by which he is environed. He knows that for him, and for all men, the will of God is supreme. He has, therefore, the power and habit of forming a just judgment on wealth and poverty, joy and sorrow, ease and pain, public honour and public dishonour, and all the incidents of human experience. He has a clear vision of the laws which should regulate conduct, and of the principles which form the character.

This is the wisdom of which James gives an account. It is '*first pure*'—a word which, as Bishop Westcott says, 'suggests the notion of shrinking from contamination, of a delicate sensibility to pollution of any kind.'[1] Conscience, even in Christian men, is too often wanting in sensitiveness; they avoid the grosser sins, but have no fine and subtle sense to recognise sins of a less flagrant kind. They are constantly approaching too near the line which separates evil from good. They do not instinctively keep as far away from it as they can. They try to escape dark and ugly stains on their character; but they forget that the nations of the

[1] Westcott, *The First Epistle of John* (iii. 3), p. 98.

saved in the City of God walk in white raiment, and that even the dust of the common earth shows on it and destroys its shining purity. '*The wisdom that cometh from above is first pure.*'

It is also '*peaceable.*' That is an excellent test whether the teaching which a man thinks he has received from God really came from God or not. Does it make him contentious and aggressive? Or, even while he is endeavouring to prevail upon Christian men to receive a truth which they regard with suspicion and distrust, is it clear that his affection for them is unbroken, and that he dreads the prevalence of bitterness and ill-temper among Christian people as much as he dreads the power of error? Is it manifest that he does not suppose his clearer vision of some great truth impairs the worth of all that his brethren had known of that truth before—that he does not imagine that their claim to be regarded as loyal to Christ is lessened by the error which, as he thinks, he has discovered in their creed? Does he teach, or does he fight? Does he imply that the new truth which he has to tell gives him some personal distinction? Lord Bolingbroke said of Fénelon that 'the Archbishop never *outshone*, but would lead you into truths in such a manner that you thought you discovered them yourself.'[1] What a wonderful contrast to the insolent contempt for all who do not accept their opinions which characterises some public speakers. The mere profession of

[1] Spence's *Anecdotes*, p. 23.

brotherly affection for those from whom we differ is not enough. Do we actually treat them as brothers, and as brothers whom we love? Some of you may remember Cardinal Newman, in his reply to Dr. Pusey's *Eirenicon*, said, 'You have discharged your olive branch from a catapult'; and there are some professions of a peaceable disposition which are more aggressive and exasperating than a declaration of war.

Of course the time may come when it will be necessary to fight. If after making known the truth, or what seems to us the truth, in the most peaceable manner, it is fiercely assailed, grossly misrepresented, then controversy may become inevitable. But even in controversy, and in very resolute and strenuous controversy, it is possible to preserve and to show a kindly and peaceable spirit; a desire not to exaggerate differences, not to charge men with necessarily holding the logical inferences from their opinions when they repudiate these inferences; not to dwell with exulting mockery on accidental errors of statement, or on arguments which are flagrantly inconclusive; not to import into the discussion of great questions mere irrelevant personalities. Above all, when we are engaged in controversy with Christian men, the wisdom which is '*from above*,' and which is '*peaceable*,' will never allow us to forget that they are brethren in Christ.

Wisdom—the true wisdom—is '*gentle*.' The gentleness which James attributes to it is that perfection and grace on which Mr. Matthew Arnold had so much to say, and to which he gave the name of 'sweet reasonableness.' Mr. Arnold says that 'This mildness and sweet reasonableness it was, which, stamped with the individual charm they had in Jesus Christ, came into the world as something new, won its heart and conquered it. Every one had been asserting his ordinary self and was miserable; to forbear to assert one's ordinary self, to place one's happiness in mildness and sweet reasonableness, was a revelation.'[1] He thought, and had good reason for thinking, that all of us are greatly wanting in it. Aristotle in a passage quoted by Mr. Mayor in his *Commentary*, has a charming description of this virtue.[2] In his Ethics he contrasts it with strict justice; in his Rhetoric he gives a more detailed account of it. Translators differ as to the best English equivalent for its name. Grant gives 'equity.' 'It is equity,' said Aristotle, 'to pardon human failings, and to look to the lawgiver and not to the law, to the spirit and not to the letter, to the intention and not to the action, to the whole and not to the part, to the character of the actor in the long-run and not in the present moment, to remember good rather than evil, and good that one has received rather than good that one has done, to put up with injurious treatment, to wish to settle a matter by words rather than by deeds, lastly, to prefer arbitration to judgment,'—that is, a judgment in the courts.

[1] Arnold: *St. Paul and Protestantism*, p. xix. [2] Mayor, pp. 122, 123.

This, I say, is what James calls the '*gentleness*,' or '*meekness*,' of wisdom, and what Mr. Arnold calls 'sweet reasonableness.' Try to imagine the change which would pass upon human life if this virtue were common, were universal. How much that irritates and wounds and leaves a rankling sense of injustice would disappear! How few would be the friendships that we should lose, how few the enmities that we should create! It is a virtue that should appear in our intercourse with our equals and our superiors; but it is especially a virtue to be illustrated in our relations to those over whom we have more or less authority; and if in the relations of masters and mistresses to those in their employment, of foremen to workmen, of the old to the young, of parents to children, there were this gentleness, this equity, this sweet reasonableness, how different would be the atmosphere and temper of our places of business and our homes!

Wisdom is '*easy to be entreated*.' The phrase has such beauty in it that I feel reluctant to make any attempt to explain its meaning. It describes a temper the opposite of self-will, self-assertion, obstinacy. This too is a virtue to be shown towards persons of every description. But as '*gentleness*,' 'sweet reasonableness,' finds its most excellent and gracious expression in our relations to those over whom we have some kind of authority, this virtue has its special exercise in our relations to those who have some kind of authority over us. One ancient author says that he alone has this virtue who 'willingly,' not reluctantly, 'submits to a true fatherly will.'[1] The word is often used to describe the temper which submits easily and cheerfully to military discipline. Mr. Mayor thinks that it might fairly be translated by the words 'submissive, docile, tractable.'[2]

I cannot tell whether this virtue is common or uncommon. Many of you have better means of knowing than I have. Nor can I tell whether it is less or more common that it used to be. As it is a virtue of educated, as distinguished from untaught and undisciplined men, of a civilised people, as distinguished from barbarian, it ought to be more common in our days than it was in past times. But in the course of my life I have met with a considerable number of persons in whose character it was absent, and whose worth as members of the social order was greatly lessened by its absence,—persons who found it intolerable to recognise any authority over them, to obey orders, to give an account of themselves and of their work to those whose right and duty it was to require it, who resented, sometimes passionately, sometimes sullenly, all interference on the part of their parents, or of those who employed them, or who were responsible for their work. I have known persons who would refuse to do a thing simply because they were asked to do it, and who would have done it cheerfully if they had not been asked; persons who, if requested

[1] Musconius, quoted by Mayor, p. 123. [2] Mayor, *l.c.*

to do a thing in one way, would be certain to do it in another, who seemed incapable of following directions, which, had they followed them, would have saved both themselves and other people a great deal of annoyance. They are always putting grit in the wheels of every machine that they touch. I should not at all wonder if there are people in this city, who, because the Town Council ask them to keep to the right, persistently keep to the left. There are men who seem unable to learn that if we are to live together in any kind of society, whether a family, a city, a nation, or a Church, some arrangements must be made by responsible persons, and that the arrangements should be loyally accepted, even though they may not see the reasons for them. This incapacity to keep in the ranks, to walk in the road and not trespass, to do as other people do, is shown in many odd ways. If there is a collection for the General Hospital, these excellent people send in a special contribution for the Queen's. If the congregation to which they belong supports the London Missionary Society, they subscribe to the Inland China Mission, or to a special Mission on the Congo. They forget that we are members one of another, and that hearty co-operation is necessary if the life of the Church is to be vigorous and its work effectively done. We should learn to care for the things for which our brethren care, and should make our strength and resources theirs. We should not stand apart from them for the mere sake of standing apart, or to gratify a personal preference and taste, or do things in our own way when we can do it in their way, and so increase the efficiency of their service. We are, I repeat, members one of another.

'*Full of mercy and good fruits.*' There is a kind of wisdom which is often called a knowledge of the world, which makes men cynical and hardens their hearts against the appeals of misfortune, of weakness, of error, of sin. Sympathy, forbearance, and generosity, so they say, can do nothing to lessen the follies and miseries of the world. Help a man to-day—he will be equally in want of help next week. Pass over a man's fault to-day—he will commit it again within a month. What is the use of taking trouble to relieve the distress of people, whose weaknesses, or whose vices will always prevent them from living a quiet and prosperous life? Such men will say very shrewd things about the real causes of the sufferings of vast masses of men, but will do nothing to lessen them; will speculate on the laws which make some nations, some individuals, prosperous, but upon other nations, other individuals, bring great calamities; and the only conclusion from their speculation is, that while there is a great deal of weakness and vice and misery in the world, nothing can be done to make the race stronger, wiser, better, happier.

This wisdom, however profound it may appear, is not, according to James, the wisdom that '*cometh from above.*' It comes from a wide and thoughtful observation of mankind, not from fellowship with God. It leaves God out of account, and therefore despairs of man. But the true wisdom—the wisdom which God gives—looks upon men in the light of God, bears with their sins, pities their sorrows, is strenuous in the endeavour to relieve their sufferings, and to form them to the habits of a virtuous, honourable, and Christian life. It is '*full of mercy and good fruits.*'

'*Without variance.*' That is a phrase, which to my mind at least conveys no meaning, and yet perhaps it is the best which the Revisers could have chosen. Nor is it at all easy to discover what the word which it is intended to represent stands for. It is a word about which New Testament scholars are much perplexed. I venture to suggest that its meaning may be discovered by considering the contrast in one very important particular between what is called worldly wisdom, and the wisdom which cometh *from above.* The man whose conduct is governed by worldly wisdom is apt to be shifty—what he himself would call politic. He sets his sails to the prevailing wind; speaks well of men to-day of whom he spoke ill yesterday—not because the men themselves are better than they were, but because yesterday he could get nothing by speaking well of them, and to-day he can. His very judgment of men is determined by his interests or his passions; and since with changing circumstances his interests and his passions vary, his judgment varies too. You can never count upon him. But the man who is governed by divine wisdom has his fixed principles, and by these both his judgment and his conduct are ruled. He looks upon human affairs from divine heights. The compass which guides his course is not deflected from its true meridian by the attraction of self-interest, or by the varying currents of prevailing opinion. He judges men to-day as he judged them yesterday,—unless indeed he has learnt new facts about them which require him to modify his judgment. He does not think better of them simply because they have become rich and powerful and able to help him, or worse of them because they have become poor, and have lost their riches and are unable to help him any longer. He does not treat them differently for any such reasons as these. He maintains that true consistency which comes not from an obstinate adherence to his own opinions, but from persistent loyalty to the high and eternal principles by which human conviction and human conduct should be governed. This, I think, suggests that quality of divine wisdom which is described by the word represented by the phrase '*without variance*.'

'*Without hypocrisy*.' That phrase needs no explanation. Worldly wisdom may often make a man a hypocrite, may lead him to flatter men whom he despises, to profess a zeal for opinions in which he has no serious belief, to affect generosity and public spirit, when he is only seeking personal consideration and advancement; but the man who has the wisdom which cometh '*from above*,' always takes God into account, and to him hypocrisy is impossible.

To James this wisdom is a divine gift. It '*cometh down from above*.' It is not to be acquired by any experience of human life, by the largest and most thoughtful observation of the ways and fortunes of men. If a man lacks this wisdom, he is to '*ask of God, who giveth to all men liberally, and upbraideth not*.'

He closes the passage with a characteristic and most suggestive apothegm. How are we to become righteous ourselves, to be faithful to duty, under difficult and perplexing and irritating conditions? How are we to induce other men to act righteously, to really become righteous; or to use the figure which James employs—how are we to get from the soil of human life a '*harvest of righteousness*'? James answers that this harvest must be '*sown in peace*,' and it will be reaped by those whose spirit and temper make peace. '*The fruit of righteousness is sown in peace for them that make peace*.' Not through a fierce and angry temper, by which we ourselves are liable to be betrayed into gross injustice and into many other sins, and which will also provoke other men to sin, but by gentleness, kindness, peaceableness, will righteousness at last come to prevail. Or as James says elsewhere, '*The wrath of man worketh not the righteousness of God*.'

X

CHRISTIAN WORLDLINESS

'*Whence come wars and whence come fightings among you? come they not hence, even of your pleasures that war in your members? Ye lust, and have not: ye kill, and covet, and cannot obtain: ye fight and war; ye have not, because ye ask not. Ye ask and receive not, because ye ask amiss, that ye may spend it in your pleasures. Ye adulteresses, know ye not that the friendship of the world is enmity with God? Whosoever therefore would be a friend of the world maketh himself an enemy of God. Or think ye that the scripture speaketh in vain? Doth the spirit which He made to dwell in us long unto envying? But He giveth more grace.*'—JAMES iv. 1-6.

THESE are stirring words; there is a fierceness in them which recalls the severity and passion with which the prophets denounced the sins of the Jewish people in the worst times of their history. At the close of the preceding chapter James had said, '*The fruit of righteousness is sown in peace for them that make peace.*' But among these Jewish Christians settled on the great plains between the Euphrates and Tigris, to whom the Epistle was specially addressed, there was very little of the peaceable spirit, and as soon as James has written the word '*peace*' he breaks out into vehement reproaches. There are '*wars and fightings*' among them,—lasting enmities, angry rivalries and contests. Whence did they come?

'*Come they not hence, even of your pleasures that war in your members?*' The word '*members*' stands for all those inferior powers of human nature which ought to be under the control of the conscience and the reason, but which too often become ungovernable and betray men into sin. These powers render us capable of many transient pleasures, and the desire for these pleasures may become so strong and vehement as to escape from the moral control by which it ought to be regulated. James represents the '*pleasures*'—or the desires which have these pleasures for their object—as encamped in our members, and as originating and sustaining the enmities and quarrels which he is condemning.

'*Ye lust and have not*': that is, they desired pleasant things which they could not gain; they wanted wealth, they wanted office, they wanted public consideration and honour. Whatever good things they saw in the possession of other men, they passionately wished to have themselves. '*Ye kill*':—that is a startling and almost incredible charge; and so some expositors soften the meaning of the word, and suggest that what James meant was that they had the spirit of murderers; they hated with deadly hatred men who were more prosperous than themselves. His words recall what John said in his Epistle many years later, 'He that hateth his brother is a murderer: and ye know that no murderer hath eternal life abiding in him.'[1] But I am inclined to

[1] 1 John iii. 15.

take the word literally. In their reckless and unscrupulous endeavours to obtain office and wealth, they ruined the fortunes and broke the hearts of those who stood in their way—reduced them to beggary—practically killed them.

But whether we attach this meaning to the word, or suppose that James intended simply to say that they hated others with a murderous hatred, there is a certain bathos in saying '*Ye murder*,'—or have the spirit of murder,—'*ye covet and cannot obtain*.' Mr. Mayor suggests what seems to me a very desirable change in the punctuation. He would read, '*Ye lust and have not—ye kill: ye covet* (or *are jealous*) *and cannot obtain—ye fight and war*!'[1] That makes the passage impressive and vigorous. They had a great desire for the good things of this life, but could not get them, and in their fierceness, without intending to do it, they killed their rivals. They were jealous of people who were more fortunate and more prosperous and more distinguished than themselves; they struggled fiercely to get their fame, or their business, or their office, or their honours. It is a miserable description of the temper of Christian men; it startles us to find that such a temper should have been possible in Christian churches within twenty years after the death and resurrection of our Lord. No wonder that 'the brother of our Lord' condemned it sternly and vehemently.

He goes on to say that they had no rest of heart

[1] Mayor, pp. 125-127.

—no satisfaction in life—because they did not pray; '*Ye have not because ye ask not.*' Or if they asked, they did not receive, because they asked badly,—entreated God to satisfy their covetousness, their ambition, their love of luxury and ease; '*Ye ask amiss, that ye may spend it in your pleasures.*'

Then follows a vehement passage suggested by a conception of the relationship between God and Israel, familiar to the writers of the Old Testament. Israel is represented in the Old Testament as the Bride of Jehovah; and when Israel fell away from fidelity to Him and worshipped heathen gods, the crime is represented as the crime of adultery; Israel had been faithless to her vows. And now James declares that the Christian people to whom he is writing had been guilty of a similar offence. In ancient Israel the worship of heathen gods is adultery; in the Christian Church friendship with the world is adultery. '*Ye adulteresses, know ye not that the friendship of the world is enmity with God? Whosoever therefore would be a friend of the world maketh himself an enemy of God.*

These words raise a question which goes to the very root of the practical life of every one of us. In past generations, Christian people—our own fathers—were conscious of a strong contrast between the Church and the world; between those who are in Christ and those who are not; between those who are endeavouring, whatever may be their imperfections and failures, to get the will of God done on earth as it is done in heaven, and those who are not; between those who are under the power of God's invisible and eternal kingdom and those who are not.

Our ecclesiastical ancestors were in the habit of condemning in Christian men, not merely actions and habits which they regarded as immoral, but actions and habits which they regarded as 'worldly.' They did not believe that all questions of conduct could be determined by what we commonly describe as the moral law. As I have said, they were far more distinctly conscious of the contrast between the 'Church' and the 'World' than we are; far more distinctly conscious of the difference between the life which should be lived by a man who in the power of his union with the risen and glorified Christ has already passed into the Kingdom of Heaven, and the noblest life which can be lived by those who have not received that great deliverance. They therefore had a great deal to say—not merely about what is morally right and what is morally wrong, but about what is worldly and what is unworldly. In the conduct of life they had to take into account their relations to God and to the invisible and eternal order as well as to human society.

All of us who have passed middle life can remember when there was very much more preaching about 'worldliness' in our pulpits than there is now, and when questions about 'worldliness' were more eagerly discussed by Christian people in private conversation. The very word seems now to have gone almost out of use. Christian men are anxious to avoid what is morally wrong, but they appear to have ceased to be anxious to avoid 'worldliness.'

Those frequent discussions which some of us can recall, when we look back thirty or forty years, as to whether particular acts and particular habits were 'worldly' or not, indicated, I think, that the true idea of worldliness and of unworldliness had almost disappeared; for worldliness is a quality of temper and life, and not a mere question of particular acts or habits,—not, at any rate, a question of such particular acts or habits as those which were most frequently the subject of dispute. The discussions also indicated that already there was restlessness and impatience among Christian people under that rule of life which was imposed by the traditions of our Churches, and which distinguished between what was 'worldly' and what was not. Some of those restraints had indeed become obsolete and unmeaning. For example, it was supposed to be 'worldly' to play at billiards, but the most eminent 'professor' incurred no censure by playing at bagatelle. If a pack of cards was seen in a house, it was a clear proof that the family was 'worldly'; but chess and draughts—and I think dominoes—were not inconsistent with shining piety. Scott's novels, which are tales in prose, were forbidden; Scott's poems, which are tales in verse, were permitted. Young people began to feel that there was a want of reality in these distinctions, and with that presumption which must be forgiven to youthful inexperience, they began to mock at them, and to talk as if their grandfathers and great-grandfathers must have been fools to institute and to observe them. But if we come to think of it, we shall see that there was a considerable amount of genius in the world, and of intellectual vigour, and of penetration, and of subtlety, before any of us were born. And there was also a deep and strong faith in God, and a sense of the infinite contrast between right and wrong, and a serious, earnest desire to live the perfect life. If, therefore, some of the restrictions on conduct which we inherited from the past, but which have now almost vanished, seem childish and unmeaning, humility and a true knowledge of the kind of men our fathers were will silence our mockery, and will lead us to ask how it happened that wise and strong and able men originated and observed them. In most cases a clear answer can be given. Take, for example, bagatelle and billiards. In the early part of this century very few middle-class houses had a billiard table; it is an expensive piece of furniture, and it requires a room to itself. If people wanted to play billiards, they had nearly always to go to a public table; and the public table was usually at an inn or an hotel, and with the billiards there was often—on the part at least of those who watched the game, and on the part of the players when it was over—more drinking of brandy and water than was good for them, and in the billiard-room gambling of a more or less serious kind was also not uncommon. But people with a modest income, and living in a modest house, could have a bagatelle-board of their own, could put it on the dining-room table in the evening, and father and mother, brothers and sisters, could play together. Our fathers and grandfathers and great-grandfathers who allowed bagatelle and forbade billiards were not fools.

But it was not merely in their amusements that our ecclesiastical forefathers were under restraint. A wealthy man who had inherited the traditions of our Churches would, as a matter of course, live in a smaller house than most men of the 'world' with an equal income; would keep fewer servants, and fewer horses and carriages; would have fewer courses on his table at dinner, and give less costly entertainments. His wife and daughters would dress less fashionably and less expensively than ladies of the 'world' that were of the same social position. 'Unworldliness' was supposed to require simplicity and modesty, an abstinence from ostentation and luxury in methods of living. To lay down rules as to what is permissible and what is forbidden in matters of this kind was not possible. I suppose that there are some observances and customs which are maintained as matters of course in the palaces of kings which would be ostentatious in the house of a duke. For the family of a great nobleman whose ancestors fought in the Wars of the Roses, simplicity of living would be one thing; for the family of a respectable tradesman, who in his early years had thought himself fortunate when he secured a situation with a salary of two hundred a year, simplicity of living would be a very different thing. But though no definite rules could be laid down, the instincts and traditions of our churches exerted at one time a very effective control over the conduct of their members, and disciplined them to avoid all unnecessary and ostentatious expenditure. The late Mr. Walter Bagehot was told that a friend of his was engaged to be married. 'Who is the lady?' he asked. 'A Dissenter,' was the reply. 'Ah!' he said, 'that is right; she will have money.' He knew that the simple and modest methods of life among hereditary Nonconformists of the middle classes led naturally to the accumulation of wealth.

In that direction lay their peril. When the ardour of the great days of Nonconformity had cooled, and 'worldliness' was identified with the violation of certain external rules of conduct, the Nonconformist forgot that the counting-house in which he spent the greater part of his life might be more fatal to 'unworldliness' than an occasional evening at the theatre; exciting speculations in sugar, in cotton, or in corn, than an exciting run with the hounds; his ledger, his bank book, and his yearly balance sheet than all the Waverley novels.

'Unworldliness' does not consist in the most rigid and conscientious observance of any external rules of conduct, but in the spirit and temper and in the habit of living, created by the vision of God, by constant fellowship with Him, by a personal and vivid experience of the greatness of the Christian redemption, by the settled purpose to do the will of God always, in all things, at all costs, and by the power of the great hope—the full assurance—that, after our mortal years are spent, there is a larger, fuller, richer, loftier life in His immediate and eternal Presence.

It is true, I repeat, that the tests by which our forefathers determined whether men belonged to the one class or to the other, were often technical and artificial, and that they often failed to see that the same divine life might manifest itself under very different forms. It is also true that they drew the line between the true Church and the world too sharply and too confidently; for there is a wide borderland between the two hostile powers, and for us it is not possible to be certain of the boundary between them. There are vast multitudes of men about whom we cannot be sure whether they have really received the life of God, though in their tastes and temper and character they have been largely influenced by the faith and spirit of the Church; or whether they are destitute of the life of God, though in their habits and aims and principles of conduct they are too much under the control of the world. But in their main contention our fathers were wholly in the right; the Church—the true

Church—and the world are in irreconcileable opposition to each other. The Church is on the side of God, and the world is against Him. '*Whosoever therefore would be a friend of the world, maketh himself an enemy of God.*'

These are very serious words, and it is to be feared that in the case of large numbers of Christian people the truth which they affirm exerts a very inadequate influence over the practical conduct of life. We all avoid, as a matter of course, intimate association with men who are guilty of flagrant vices,—guilty of drunkenness, sensual sins, habitual lying, dishonesty, gross profanity. We have no desire to be on good terms with them; we should feel it to be a disgrace to be called their friends; we do not wish that they should have a good opinion of us. But all of us come into contact, more or less close, with people who, without being vicious, are in the real and true sense of the word, 'worldly.' In their business, in their pleasures, in their homes, in their personal habits, the authority of God has no place; they belong to a vast unorganised society whose whole life is withdrawn from His control. They do nothing to win His approval; they abstain from doing nothing to escape His condemnation. They may profess the Christian creed, or they may reject it; but in either case it has no effective power over their conduct. They have no sense of the evil of sin, no dread of judgment to come, no joy in the infinite grace of God and in all that He has done for the redemption of the world through Christ. They think nothing of the infinite hopes of those who see beyond death endless ages of righteousness and blessedness in the presence of God. It never occurs to them to lay up treasure in Heaven. They may be anxious for the approval of their own conscience; but they never seriously ask whether they are so living as to have God's approval. They may be kindly and generous, and may give time and strength and money to relieving the miseries of the wretched and improving their material condition; but they never think of men as having any capacities for joy and sorrow, honour and shame, beyond the limits of these mortal years. They may have a keen interest in all the creations of human genius and in the discoveries of science; they may do a great deal to elevate and enrich the intellectual lives of others; but they themselves care nothing for the knowledge of God, and of course they do nothing to extend that knowledge to other men. And so, whether they are living what may be called an earnest, a vigorous, and an honourable life, or a life that is vain and frivolous, it is a life wholly controlled and determined by this world. In their aims and hopes, in their joys and sorrows, in the laws which govern their conduct, there is nothing drawn from faith in God, from love for Christ, from the vision of things unseen and eternal. We all come into contact with such men. They naturally draw to each other, and they confirm each other in their practical disregard of God and all the higher interests of human life. They belong to the 'world'; they are resisting, consciously or unconsciously, the power of the revelation of God which has come to us through our Lord Jesus Christ. The saints of every generation are on one side,—they are on another. While they continue as they are—and they help each other to continue as they are—the great purpose for which Christ came into the world—the restoration of all men to God—will be thwarted and delayed. Is it not clear that '*whosoever would be a friend of the world maketh himself an enemy of God*'?

With the world, as a vast society of men who are living without any real regard for God, the Christian man can never desire to be on good terms. To individuals who belong to it he may be strongly drawn. They may be honourable men of business, excellent colleagues in public and philanthropic work, pleasant and kindly in their spirit. He may see much in them to esteem, much to imitate; but the power which they represent is a power opposed to God, and he cannot be its friend. And even with excellent and exemplary men of the world he will often find himself ill at ease. As soon as their intercourse passes to the deeper elements and more serious aspects of life, he will be conscious that in all his judgments of human affairs he has to appeal to an authority to which they are indifferent; that they care nothing for precisely those things for which he cares most; that he and they live in wholly different realms of life. He will not, if he is faithful to Christ, attempt to conciliate their friendship by affecting their speech and talking as though his thoughts of human life were no higher and deeper than theirs. Nor will he, in his personal habits and the ordering of his home, be influenced by their example, rather than by the spirit and principle of his Christian faith and by his hope of eternal glory; nor will he, when he and they happen to be together, omit any Christian duty for the sake of not giving them offence. He will live his own life,—the life which he believes will please God,—though they may think it singular and eccentric, and may be repelled by it. He will see that to wish to be and to try to be a '*friend of the world*' is to make himself '*an enemy of God.*'

The passage which follows is for several reasons a difficult one; but by a little effort and patience we may come to see its meaning.

'*Or think ye that the scripture speaketh in vain? Doth the spirit which he made to dwell in us long unto envying?*' The second alternative reading given in the margin seems a better expression of the thought: '*Or think ye that the scripture speaketh in vain? that spirit which he made to dwell in us yearneth for us even unto jealous envy.*'

The first difficulty arises from the fact that these words do not occur in any part of the Old Testament. But James may not have meant to imply that the precise words were found in the Old Testament; he may only have meant that there were passages that spoke of the divine jealousy; and of these there are many. In the second Commandment, the Jewish people are forbidden to make graven images of any form that is in heaven above, or that is in the earth beneath, or that is in the water under the earth: 'Thou shalt not bow down thyself to them, nor serve them: for I the Lord thy God am a jealous God.'[1] Heathen races worshipped many gods in many temples with many rites; their deities were not supposed to regard the practice with any disapproval. But Jehovah will not tolerate devotion to any other gods; He will be the solitary object of worship in Israel; He is 'a jealous God.' In the great Song of Moses in Deuteronomy, Moses recalls the sins of the people in the desert, and says: 'They provoked Him to jealousy with strange gods.'[2] I might quote other passages, but it is unnecessary. With us the word 'jealousy' has evil associations, but it may stand for a passion which is absolutely right and honourable. There are human relations in which we have a right to feel pain and anger at the alienation from us of an affection, a devotion, and a confidence, which are our due. There is a petty jealousy which is base, selfish, and contemptible; but there is also a jealousy which is inseparable from a generous and ardent love. Mr. Mayor's free translation of this passage liberates it from all that is mean and ignoble: 'The Spirit which He made to dwell in us jealously yearns for the entire

[1] Exodus xx. 5. [2] Deut. xxxii. 16.

devotion of the heart.'[1] In that entire devotion of the heart to God lies the root of all Christian perfection, and it is necessary to the peace and joy of the Christian life. God cannot but be grieved when it is withheld. The grief has an element of generous resentment in it; it is jealousy,—but a jealousy without sullenness, without bitterness, and desiring no revenge. It is the pain of an infinite love which is thwarted and repelled in its desire to bless men with perfect righteousness and perfect joy. Let the erring heart be troubled for a moment by the increasing distance between itself and God,—let there be any wistful and sorrowful thoughts of a lost blessedness, any impulse, however faint, to repentance,—and God will abundantly pardon. His jealousy did but disclose the depth and strength of His love for us; and now the greatness of His love is the measure of the goodness and bounty that He will show to the penitent. Had He cared nothing for us, or cared little, there would have been no jealousy when we rejected Him. But when we repent, the very passion of His love, which is revealed in the jealousy, will move Him to give '*more grace*.' Let there be no resentment, therefore, against the exactingness of God's claims on us. It is the exactingness of an infinite love, which cannot be content with anything less than our complete restoration to the image of the Divine holiness, and our perfect fellowship with the Divine joy. That

[1] Mayor, p. 132.

which God asks for He gives. If He requires from us an absolute and complete devotion to Himself, it is because He is ready to grant us the power of His Spirit to create and to sustain that devotion in our hearts. Every precept is but the reverse of a promise; every command is but the prophecy of a grace. The loftier His commands the larger His bounty. Augustine summed up this truth in the words: 'Give what Thou askest, and then ask what Thou wilt.' Should not that be the temper and spirit we should always cultivate in the presence of God? He may ask from us any service, any endurance; only first He gives that which He asks—power to serve and power to endure. God does give to those willing to receive it all the grace necessary for every need.

PART II

XI

THE TWO GOSPELS

'I live; and yet no longer I, but Christ liveth in me.'
GALATIANS ii. 20.

IF these words stood alone, we might regard them as an illustration of rhetoric made gloriously intense by passion. Translated into cooler and more exact terms, their meaning could in that case be expressed in some such way as this: Paul meant that the revelation of the grace and righteousness of God in Christ had taken complete possession of him; had filled his whole mind; had displaced all his previous beliefs or transfigured them; had kindled his imagination; had inspired him with a devotion to Christ which drew into itself all the passions and forces of his life, so that he had wholly ceased to care for those things which were once dear to him and were still dear to other men,—a devotion so absolute that he had now no other desire, or hope, or joy, or aim, than to do the will of Christ, and contribute whether by action or suffering to those great ends for which Christ Himself lived and died, and rose again and ascended to the Father.

If, I say, the words stood alone, this might be an adequate account of them. We might say that Paul meant that he was so mastered by the vision of the grace and glory of Christ's own perfection, and by what Christ had revealed of the Father, that all personal interests and aims had passed away like flax at the touch of fire, and that his life was so completely surrendered to Christ and the service of Christ that it might be said that Christ lived in him.

But the words do not stand alone, and this is an inadequate explanation of their meaning. Paul meant exactly what he said—*Christ lived in him.* He was not merely under the power of the vision of Christ's perfection; nor was he merely under the power of the revelation which Christ had made of God's grace and righteousness. He was conscious of a very wonderful personal union between himself and Christ: '*I live; and yet no longer I, but Christ liveth in me.*'

There is a memorable and impressive passage in Cardinal Newman's story of his early religious experience which will, perhaps, enable us to see Paul's meaning more clearly. When he was about fifteen years old he passed through a great religious change; and one of the first books which he read was a work of Romaine's, from which he learnt the Calvinistic doctrine of final perseverance,—which, it is hardly necessary to say, he has since rejected. He says,[1] 'I received it at once, and believed that the inward conversion of which I was conscious (and of which I still am more certain than that I have hands or feet), would last into the next life, and that I was elected to

[1] Newman, *Apologia*, p. 4.

eternal glory.' This belief, which he retained for some years, had, he thinks, some influence on his opinions and life, especially—to quote his own words—'in isolating me from the objects which surrounded me, in confirming me in my mistrust of the reality of material phenomena, and making me rest in the thought of two and two only absolute and luminously self-evident beings, myself and my Creator.' I am sure that this impressive passage does not contain a complete account of Cardinal Newman's highest spiritual experiences, even in those early years; but I have quoted his words because they happen to express what some devout persons suppose to be an adequate representation of the perfect ideal of the spiritual life. This is what they desire. If they could rise to this height they would be content. There is nothing to be hoped beyond it. 'Two—and two only—absolute and luminously self-evident beings, myself and my Creator': the words touch their imagination; surely the hours when the soul is conscious of itself and of God—of itself and God only—are the great hours of life.

But if Cardinal Newman's words are taken without addition, without explanations, they express a conception of the spiritual order of the world wholly different from that which is revealed in Christ and in the teaching of Christ,—wholly different, too, from that which is illustrated in the personal life of the Christian apostles. 'Two and two only supreme and luminously self-evident beings, myself and my Creator':

this assumes that in his relations to the Eternal every man stands apart and alone; that he meets God in the power or the weakness of his own personal life; that what he himself is determines the clearness of his vision of God, and the measure of his blessedness in God. He may have received many aids to perfection—the discipline of temptation, of service, of sorrow, of joy. In the Lord Jesus Christ he may have found revelations of the Divine majesty and affecting proofs of the Divine grace. He may have had the support of mysterious influences of the Divine Spirit. But all these have only contributed to the strength and sanctity of his personal life, and now he stands, as I have said, apart and alone, in the presence of God.

Paul's account of himself is very different: '*I live; and yet no longer I, but Christ liveth in me.*' 'Blessed be the God and Father of our Lord Jesus Christ, who hath blessed us with every spiritual blessing in the heavenly places in Christ.'[1] John's account of the ideal life is very different: 'We know that the Son of God is come, and hath given us an understanding, that we know Him that is true, and we are in Him that is true, even in His Son Jesus Christ.'[2] Our Lord's own account of the true spiritual order is very different: 'I am the Vine, ye are the branches.'[3] The central principle of the Christian Gospel—its characteristic power—is in direct antagonism to this theory of individualism in its extreme form. The individual man does not, according to God's thought

[1] Ephesians i. 3. [2] 1 John v. 20. [3] John xv. 5.

and purpose, stand in God's presence alone, apart, in his own isolated strength. We are unequal to worship, and unequal to the claims of common Christian duty, unless we, like Paul, are able to say, '*I live; yet no longer I, but Christ liveth in me.*'

And the acceptance or rejection of that truth does not merely affect a man's conception of particular Christian doctrines and the method of the spiritual life; it reaches very far: accept it frankly, with all that it involves, and you have one conception of the Christian Gospel; reject it, and you have quite another conception.

I want to bring out, point by point, some of the contrasts between these two conceptions—these two Gospels. The root of the whole difference between them consists, I repeat, in this: one of them assumes that in the spiritual order, and in his relations to God, every man is, and must be, an absolutely separate and isolated personality; the other denies this, and affirms that, according to the true order of the spiritual world, the life and personality of every man are rooted in the Eternal Son of God, who became flesh for us sinners and for our salvation.

I

Let us consider these two conceptions of the Gospel: In the first place, in relation to the forgiveness of sin. According to the one conception, which assumes that every man stands in the presence of God apart and alone,—according to this conception of the Gospel, Christ came into the world to create a new and most powerful set of spiritual forces by which sinful men are to be moved to repentance, strengthened to break with their evil life, and drawn to trust in God's mercy. There—so far as the forgiveness of sin is concerned—the grace of Christ reaches its end. He became incarnate; He worked miracles; He spoke to men of God's infinite goodness and love; He died an awful death; and by all that He was, all that He did, all that He said, all that He suffered, He appeals to every man to repent and to trust in God to forgive him. I repeat that according to this conception of the Gospel, all that Christ achieves for us, so far as the forgiveness of sin is concerned, is to surround the solitary, isolated soul with influences which encourage repentance and faith; when they have actually created repentance and faith, forgiveness follows.

That is one gospel—the gospel which assumes that every man stands in the presence of God a lonely, separate personality. Now listen to the other. The other Gospel also affirms that every man should repent of sin and forsake it, and trust in God for pardon; and it also surrounds every man with the gracious influences which should move him to repentance and inspire him with faith. But it affirms that a man need never ask whether there is enough of shame, of humiliation, of agony in his distress for past sin, enough of fortitude in his resolution to do better for the future, enough of vigour in his faith, to authorise the hope that God will be merciful; for it declares that, according to the Divine thought and purpose, he is to be eternally one with another Person,—infinitely august, —who has confessed the sin of the race, and died for it. It is for this reason—the ideal union of every man with Christ—that Christ is the Propitiation for the sin of the whole world; and therefore the relation of the whole world to God—of saint and sinner, heathen and Christian—rests on that Propitiation. In Christ, not in ourselves, we are to find the ground of the remission of sins. Christ—the Personal Christ—who is the root of all the righteousness possible to the race, is the sacrifice for the sin of the race.

But forgiveness—the cancelling of sin—is not enough. Every man whose moral and spiritual life has been raised into real and living activity desires to stand right with God, and not merely to escape Divine condemnation. The Gospel which assumes that every man lives apart and alone, finds in the revelation which has come to us through Christ the motives and powers which will enable him to achieve a personal righteousness. Through the action of these motives and these powers a man may gradually become righteous, and so at last will be in a right relation to God. The other Gospel has these same motives, these same powers, to discipline us to perfection—and, besides these, other motives and powers of a unique kind; but it declares that as soon as a man trusts in Christ, the root of his personality and life is in the Eternal Son of God. His relations to God are not determined by the righteousness of his own isolated life, for his life is not isolated—he shares the eternal relations of Christ to the Father. Christ is the ground of our justification.

Thirdly, in the pursuit of personal perfection the one Gospel teaches that Christ came to reinforce and deepen and sustain all the better elements of our separate and personal life by revelations of God which create a passion of love for Him, and give constancy to the desire and purpose to do His will. The other Gospel insists not only on this great part of the work of Christ, but affirms that we are made so completely one with Christ that the power of His life is active in our life, as the power of the life of the vine is active in all its branches. The larger Gospel does not merely contain motives to trust in God and love for Him, nor does it merely create the assured hope that the Eternal Spirit will aid the isolated soul in its endeavours to reach a consummate righteousness; it reveals the transcendent mystery of our true relation to the Lord Jesus Christ. It gives us buoyancy and courage by the discovery that Christ's will is working within our will; that the springs of our life and power lie out of ourselves, in Christ, and are therefore independent of the vacillations and uncertainties of our own personal condition. It teaches us that Christ moves us to righteousness,—not merely by pathetic and powerful motives, but by the force of His own personal energy; that He makes us strong,—not merely by adding from time to time to our own strength, but by the enduring strength of His own infinite life. And so, every one of us may come to say, '*I live; yet no longer I, but Christ liveth in me.*'

Again, the one Gospel teaches that Christ came to make known to us that we are the sons of God by creation, and to develop and strengthen the spirit of sonship by revealing to us the grace and goodness of our Heavenly Father. We are sons,—according to this Gospel,—in virtue of the separate life that dwells in every man; but, as the true idea of divine sonship includes a sharing in the moral perfection of God, Christ came to educate and discipline and train us to that perfection. The other Gospel affirms all this, but goes on to declare that God's purpose is fulfilled, not merely by the influence of His truth and of His grace on the separate and isolated soul, but by our union with His Eternal Son, in the power of whose Sonship we become, in the highest sense, sons of God.

Again, the one Gospel gives us the assurance—a great and blessed assurance—that even before we are released from the limitations of our earthly conditions we have access to God. It strengthens faith in the Divine condescension and mercy and nearness to us, by the revelations of God which are made in the teaching and earthly history of Christ, and in all that Christ has done for our race since He ascended to the Father. It also teaches us to look to the Eternal Spirit to deepen and invigorate all the affections and all the higher faculties of our spiritual nature. But then it leaves us to draw near to God alone—in the power of these revelations, and in the power of our invigorated personal life. The other Gospel gives us the same revelations of God, and assures of the same supports of the Spirit of God; but it also reveals to us that we are to find God in union with the Eternal Son of God, who is eternally one with the Father. His access to God is ours.

Again, the one Gospel gives us the exceeding great and precious promise that if, through the Divine grace, the solitary soul pursues the path of righteousness to the end, it will be received at last into the light and peace of God's eternal home, and will see His face. The other Gospel declares that in this great endeavour the soul is not solitary. It recalls with exultation the words which were spoken by Christ to His disciples the night before He suffered: 'In My Father's house are many mansions . . . I go to prepare a place for you.' 'And whither I go, ye know the way.' 'I am the Way; no one cometh unto the Father but by Me.' Our life is not lonely; we do not live apart; the great life has not to be lived in the strength of the resources which are included in the limits of our own personal existence,—even when those resources are enriched by Divine grace. We are one with Christ, and in Him we shall reach at last the blessedness and glory of God.

To sum up in a few brief sentences: The one Gospel

assumes that according to the Divine order of human life every man stands apart, and is an absolutely independent personality: that he is a separate plant, striking its own roots into the earth, revealing its own life in the power which it derives from the soil and from the gracious influences of dew and rain and light and heat. The other Gospel affirms that to fulfil the Divine order of human life, the personality of man must be rooted by man's own consent in the greater personality of Christ; that man is not a separate plant, but a branch in the Great Vine. The one Gospel assumes that since the life of man is isolated, he is to reach perfection by his personal endeavour, by self-culture, through the discipline of sorrow and joy and service, in the power of all that he can learn concerning the awful greatness, the perfect holiness, and the infinite love of God. It assumes that in wonderful ways the Spirit of God will act on man's isolated life, illuminating it, strengthening it, enabling it to receive and appropriate the aids to perfection given in Divine revelation, and in the infinitely varied experiences of temptation, conflict, defeat, triumph, pain, happiness, desolation,—but that the life on which all these influences are acting is still independent and self-contained. The other Gospel affirms that so long as man asserts an independent and self-contained life, he can never reach the perfection to which God has destined him, any more than a branch could bear fruit if it asserted an independent and self-contained life, and separated itself from the vine: no gracious influences of earth or heaven could enable it to bear fruit while out of the vine. The one Gospel assumes that according to the Divine order a man's relations to God are determined by the quality of his own isolated life; the other Gospel affirms that according to the Divine order our relations to God are to be determined by Christ's relations to God, and that this blessedness is achieved when, by our free consent, our personality is rooted in Christ. We are to repent; but Christ is the Propitiation for our sins: we are to live righteously; but we are justified in Christ: we are to strive for an ideal perfection; but the perfection is to reveal the quality and power of a life higher than our own, and every Christian man is to say, '*I live; yet no longer I, but Christ liveth in me*': we are to be the sons of God through sharing Christ's Sonship: we are to have access to God in the power of our union and fellowship with Christ: we are to reach the eternal home of God; but Christ is the Way to the Father, and no man cometh to the Father but by Him.

II

The Christian Gospel, in its completeness, strikes therefore at the root of an extreme and unqualified Individualism. It declares that the perfection and blessedness of man are to be found, not in the discipline and development of man's separate personal life, but by man's consent to share the life, the power, the relations to the Father, of the Lord Jesus Christ, Son of God and Saviour of the world.

Christian Faith accepts the Divine order. It is faith in Christ Himself. It acknowledges that by the Divine will there is a unique personal relation between ourselves and Him. When we on our part consent to that relation, we abandon all thought of atoning either by sorrow or by righteousness for the sins of the past, the present, or the future, and we find in Christ the propitiation for the sin of the world; we are conscious of falling far short of God's idea of righteousness, and in Christ we find justification; we despair of rising to the heights of perfection in the power of our own life; we distrust the constancy of our own will, and we rejoice to give to the will of Christ direct control over our will, and to live in the power of the life that dwells in Him; we confess that, though we were created to be the sons of God, we have fallen away from the glory to which we were destined, and we recover it by recovering our union with Christ; we are oppressed by the infinite distance between ourselves and the Eternal, and we find courage to approach Him by passing out of ourselves into Christ; we listen with wonder to revelations of the blessedness of an eternal life in God—with wonder and fear, for such a life seems infinitely beyond hope; but in becoming one with Christ, the eternal blessedness in God is ours.

It is true, indeed, that the diviner life which becomes ours through our union with Christ is but imperfectly revealed in our character and conduct. For that life has for its instrument an organisation disordered and impaired. It is like a great musician sitting at the key-board of an organ long untuned, in which many of the pipes refuse to speak and many speak falsely, and in which the action has received grave injury from damp and from unfriendly vicissitudes of temperature. His genius is baffled and thwarted. His dreams of gracious melodies and of glorious harmonies cannot be translated into actual sound. And yet sometimes there are strains of enchanting sweetness, and sometimes the chords have a divine majesty. Even when the expression of his thought is troubled and made almost inarticulate, a keen and disciplined ear can catch his wonderful meaning. No imperfections in the instrument can wholly obstruct the imperial power of the master who is handling it.

And so, while defects of intellect, infelicities of physical temperament, and a conscience which has received no wise and adequate discipline, obstruct the perfect manifestation of the grace and beauty and strength of the diviner life, there are hints and suggestions of its presence and glory. And even the rude intellect, the unlovely temperament, and the imperfectly constructed and undisciplined conscience are gradually subdued and ennobled by it. The Divine musician repairs and tunes His instrument.

III

In this account of the Christian Gospel lies the answer to many of the questions, criticisms, and difficulties which confront us in the work of foreign missions.

We are told that every race has its own intellectual methods, its own ethical ideals, its own religious impulses and cravings, and that the great ethnic religions are the natural growth of the life and traditions of the races over which they have obtained supremacy. We cannot, therefore, transfer the religious faith of Europe to Asia,—of England and Germany to China, to India, and Japan. That sounds very philosophical. But the facts are against it. The reply to it is written large across the greatest centuries of the history of the most powerful nations in the world. Asia has given a religious faith to Europe. Why may not Europe give it back to Asia? Was Christ a European? The faith and life of John—were they the fruit of Western traditions and of Western life? Was Paul an Englishman? History, I repeat—our own history—the history of all the great nations of the West—contradicts the theory that one race cannot give a faith to another whose life and traditions are wholly different from its own. Asia has given a faith to us. But the reply may be drawn from deeper sources. Not yet, even in the lands where heathenism is at its worst, has the soul of man lost its capacity for being rooted in Christ. The true life of men of every race is in Him. The differences —physical, intellectual, and ethical—by which races are contrasted with each other, do not annul their central and ultimate unity. Even the differences which may perhaps be permanent, in their intellectual conceptions of religious truth, and in the forms in which the religious life must be revealed, are consistent with their common relation to the Eternal Son of God. It is not the theology of Europe which we want the people of India or of China to receive, but the Christian Gospel of which that theology is the inadequate intellectual expression. They will create a theology for themselves which in some of its provinces will perhaps be a truer account and interpretation of Divine facts than our own. What we know for ourselves is this: man was so created that his life might be rooted in Christ; until he ceases to be man there will be something in him that will answer to the declaration that he can never know perfect peace till he find it in Another, not in himself; that he can never be strong for righteousness, until the strength of the Eternal is his.

We are told that the religious beliefs of the great nations of the East are supported by social institutions, are wrought into the organisation of families, are rooted in the traditions of thousands of years, and that they can never be changed except by an immense and awful revolution which will break up the foundations of this social order. We know the difficulties of the enterprise as well as our critics,—perhaps better; and we know our resources as they cannot know them. But to change beliefs is not the great and ultimate end of our work. We are attempting something far greater. We are attempting to change *men*,—to give them a new life, to translate them into a new world. To break down the immense structure of religious belief, religious observance, religious tradition, which has been the slow creation of millenniums—that is a task for which God has not given us the strength, nor if we had the strength should we much care to attempt it. It is a task which the millions of India and China will achieve for themselves—achieve, perhaps, very gradually, and without great public convulsions and catastrophes. It is our aim to change men, and for that greater aim strength has been given to us. We appeal to what lies deepest in their nature—the sense of incompleteness, the sense of failure, the vague craving for a richer, fuller, stronger life. We tell them that the prophecies which Christ came to fulfil are found in their dissatisfaction with themselves, their consciousness of imperfection and sin, their solicitude about what lies beyond the mystery of death. They will respond to this appeal—they are responding. If we can but make clear to them the substance of the Christian Gospel, they will answer:—'This is what we and our fathers have been waiting for: this is what we were feeling after in the darkness, if haply we might find it; the strivings, the baffled hopes, the defeats of centuries receive their interpretation in the discovery that we were made to achieve the power and perfection of our life in Christ, but till now we had not found Him.'

IV

Finally, only from this personal union with Christ can we ourselves derive enduring inspiration for this work. It is well to listen to the pathetic and passionate appeals of men whose hearts are on fire with zeal for the salvation of mankind. How deeply those appeals have sometimes moved us! Yes, and how soon has their impression passed away. If we are to have a lasting passion of love and pity for heathen nations, we must find the spring of it in Christ. Nor can we have any true conception of the height and glory of the missionary aim unless we know for ourselves the greatness of the Christian redemption. It is idle to hope that we shall ever do our part towards saving the world merely as a matter of duty; we must know how wonderful and blessed a thing it is to be saved, and this we cannot know until the mystery is revealed in our own consciousness that Christ lives in us, and that we live in Him. And for the patience which no discouragements shall weary, the courage which no difficulties shall disturb, the faith which shall rise victorious over the most disastrous defeats, to whom shall we go but to Christ? And to whom for that deep, earnest, and abiding love for men which alone will make credible what we tell them of the love of God? To whom but to Christ, who, at the impulse of an infinite love for man, descended from eternal heights of peace and glory and blessedness to abysses of confusion, darkness, and grief? And to whom for that quick sympathy which shall enable us to understand the heart of men of other races and other ways of thought, and other standards of morality than our own? To whom but to Christ, who is nearer to every man than the dearest of earthly kindred and friends—Christ, in whom we have found our Father in heaven, and in whom we may find our lost brothers and sisters on earth? Yes, this is the substance of our Gospel: every man may live a perfect life, for Christ is near to him, and Christ will live in him; and this is our inspiration and strength and support in preaching it —'*I live; yet no longer I, but Christ liveth in me.*'

XII

THE PARABLE OF THE PRODIGAL AND THE DOCTRINE OF THE ATONEMENT

LUKE XV. 11-32

I PROPOSE this evening to offer some observations on the parable of the Prodigal Son. It is perhaps the most beautiful of all the parables of Christ. He was led to deliver it by a complaint of the Pharisees and the Scribes, that when He preached publicans and sinners came to hear Him; that He actually sat down at dinner with people of that description and treated them as His friends: they thought that a man who claimed to be a prophet sent from God, and who had great tidings, as He declared, concerning the approach of the Kingdom of Heaven, should have kept Himself at a distance from disreputable men and disreputable women, and should have addressed Himself to those who professed to care for the service and honour of God. This parable is our Lord's reply to that charge. It might have been more properly called 'The Parable of the Elder Brother,' as the point of it lies in what our Lord says at the close of the parable concerning the way in which the elder brother regarded the reception of the prodigal. But the earlier part of the parable has so touched the heart and fascinated the imagination of the Church, that the point of the parable has been almost forgotten, and it has received its name, not from the elder brother of whom our Lord spoke, in order to rebuke the Scribes and Pharisees, but from the prodigal son who was received by his father with such generosity and delight.

A wealthy man is represented as dividing his property between his two sons before his death. That was not a very wise thing to do. Both his sons seem to have been the worse for it. The elder son, who remained at home, lost his reverence for his father's authority. The younger son, as soon as he received his share of the wealth, went away from home and wasted it. While his money lasted he lived a happy kind of life. It is a great mistake to suppose that all men while they are in revolt against God's authority are restless and unhappy. It is possible to forget God altogether, like this prodigal son. There are large numbers of people who are in a very far country—too far away from God to be at all troubled or disturbed by thoughts about Him. The prodigal knew that he had a father, and these people believe that they have a God. But whether his father was living or dead made no difference to the prodigal; and if it were possible for the living God to die, that would make no difference to many people. But after he had spent all he was very wretched. There was a famine; bread was dear, and his money was all gone, and now he had to try to get a miserable living by feeding swine.

His master gave him no food, and he tried to satisfy his hunger with the husks that the swine did eat. At last '*he came to himself*'; men have usually to come to themselves before they come to God. He came to himself and resolved to go home. To be a servant in his father's house would be infinitely better than to remain where he was. As soon as he made this resolution he began to fulfil it. '*He arose and came to his father.*' It would have been very natural for him to have sat watching his swine a long time before rising to go home. He must have felt what a shameful thing it was for him to have to acknowledge his sin. His father had been only too kind to him; had left him to follow his own will; had given him the command of his property before he could claim it; and he had gone away and brought disgrace on his father's name and sorrow to his father's heart. But the longer he kept away, the more he was sinning against his father. He was prolonging his father's unhappiness. And so he resolved to return. He might have said to himself that he would try to improve his condition a little before going home, that he might make a better appearance before his father when he came to him. He had sunk very low; he was miserably poor; his clothing, I suspect, was almost gone; if he went as he was, he must go in rags. Ought he not to keep away a little longer, until he could appear more decently? He knew that if he waited he might never return at all. He was in danger of perishing with hunger. He might not have strength to make the long journey before him. So at once '*he arose and came to his father*.' He might have put off going through fear that his father would not receive him. It is clear that he went without very much confidence in his father's generosity. All that he meant to ask for was that his father would put him among his hired servants. That he could have his own place in the house he did not venture to expect. But his case is so desperate, he could be no worse off, if his father refused to have anything to do with him; so '*he arose and came to his father*.' And there may be some in this congregation to-night who can discover in these successive steps in the history of the prodigal that which should guide them in their return to God. For delay, and distrust, and shame,— these keep many a man in a sinful life, who, if he only had the courage but once to return to God, would be lifted up out of the darkness into great light, and out of trouble into perfect peace. And now listen to the story of how he was received. '*While he was yet afar off, his father saw him, and was moved with compassion, and ran, and fell on his neck, and kissed him. And the son said unto him, Father, I have sinned against heaven, and in thy sight: I am no more worthy to be called thy son. But the father said to his servants, Bring forth quickly the best robe, and put it on him; and put a ring on his hand, and shoes on his feet; and bring the fatted calf, and kill it, and let us eat, and make merry: for this my son was dead, and is alive again; he was lost, and is found*.'

Now, we are sometimes told that in this parable there is nothing about the sacrifice of Christ for the sin of the world,—nothing about the Atonement. The prodigal son is forgiven by the free spontaneous mercy of his father, not on the ground of anything that had been done or suffered for him by another, and the inference is drawn that therefore the doctrine that we have redemption through the blood of Christ, even the forgiveness of sins, and that the blood of Christ was shed for the remission of sin, is a gross and injurious misrepresentation of our Lord's teaching.

I saw this put very clearly a few weeks ago in the report of a sermon on 'Forgiveness.' The preacher is represented as having said :—

'In the Parable of the Prodigal Son, they had Christ's teaching concerning sin and forgiveness, and they would have to re-write it before they got the traditional and popular theory of forgiveness out of it. There was no word there about satisfying justice before the father could receive his son. The son had borne and was bearing the punishment of his own sin, and a substitute was not required, therefore, to satisfy justice and set free the father's mercy. The teaching that contradicted that parable, no matter how widely received and confidently proclaimed, was not the truth as it is in Jesus.'

I have quoted these words because they seem to me to contain an extremely clear and a very fair statement of a very common feeling, and I ask you to consider what these words really involve. Let us see how far the principles contained in that account of the parable of the Prodigal Son will carry us. If we trust them at all, we must trust them altogether. We are told that we shall have to re-write the parable before we get the traditional and popular theory of forgiveness out of it. 'There is no word there about satisfying justice before the father could receive the son.' That is quite true, but it is a very amazing assumption that in a single parable the Lord Jesus Christ must be supposed to state the whole contents of the Christian Gospel, and that whatever this parable does not contain about the forgiveness of sins must be false. For this is the principle on which the passage I have quoted rests. There is nothing here about the Atonement, nothing about any one besides the prodigal suffering for the prodigal's sin ; therefore 'the traditional and popular' faith that Christ is the Propitiation for our sins, that He died that we might have remission of sin, 'is not the truth as it is in Jesus.'

Again I say, let us see how far these principles will carry us. There is nothing in this parable to suggest that the father took any trouble when the prodigal was in a far country to bring him to a better mood. There is nothing here to suggest that any message was sent, any entreaty, to induce the young man to come home. As far as anything in the parable is concerned, we might suppose that God left men to themselves until they were weary of their sin and resolved to return to Him ; that they returned of their own spontaneous motion, without any gracious word to encourage them to return. Shall we say, then, with the confidence of the preacher whom I have quoted, that because all this is omitted in the parable, therefore it is contrary to the parable, and not the truth as it is in Jesus?

If I contend, as I do, that the gospel is to be preached to those that are in the far country, that the assurance is to be given them that God is longing for them to return, am I to be told that the father sent no messenger to say this to the prodigal, that there is nothing in the parable about it, and therefore it is contrary to the truth that is in Jesus?

If I maintain that the Spirit of God appeals to the conscience and to the heart of men who are living in sin, recalls to them the righteousness and blessedness for which they were created, makes them restless and unhappy because they are not living their true life, am I to be told that there is nothing about all this in the parable, that the young man is represented as coming to a better mood of his own spontaneous motion, and that since there is no word about his repentance being in any sense the result of gracious influences reaching him from the father, 'the traditional and popular theory' that the Spirit of God strives with men and leads them to repentance is contrary to the truth as it is in Jesus?

In short, there is no word here of any movement of the father towards the son until the son had left the far country at his own impulse, without invitation, without encouragement, and was on his way home. The father saw him, '*when he was yet afar off,*' and then ran to meet him; though afar off, he must have travelled a long way, and must have been in sight of home. Am I to be told that that is a complete account of God's mercy? Does He do nothing for us until we have broken away from our old sin, and have made some way towards a better life? If I say that God does not forsake us when we forsake Him, does not wait till we repent before He shows us infinite goodness, does not leave us uncared for and unhelped until we have left the far country, and are returning to Him, am I to be told that there is nothing of all this in the parable, and that the teaching that contradicts the parable, 'no matter how widely received and confidently proclaimed, is not the truth as it is in Jesus'?

I have not yet done with my questions. I might ask enough to last for an hour, but I ask at least one more. For eighteen centuries the Christian Church, in all its branches, the most corrupt as well as the most pure, has preached one glorious gospel to mankind—has declared that the Son of God descended from the heights of His glory, was made flesh, and came to seek and to save the lost. This, through age after age, has been the Christian message to mankind. The fierce ambitions and rivalries of hostile churches, the confused and bitter and passionate controversies of hostile theologies, have never even in the worst times wholly suppressed or wholly concealed this wonderful gospel. It was preached in the first ages of the Church: it is preached still. It has been preached to barbarous races, to wandering tribes of men. It has been preached in cities which were the seats of imperial power, rich with the splendour of civilisation and the spoils of vanquished races. And wherever it has been preached it has touched the hearts of men to penitence, and inspired them with immortal hope. The eternal Son of God became flesh that He might seek and save the lost, and we speak of Him now as the Elder Brother of us all. He shared the infirmities, the sorrows, the temptations, the most cruel sufferings of our mortal condition, shared our poverty, our hunger, our thirst, our weariness, endured the hatred of unrelenting and powerful enemies, and the unfaithfulness of inconstant friends. One of the men whom He trusted sold Him to death for thirty pieces of silver. Perjured slanderers, bought with money of priests, swore His life away. He was condemned for blasphemy; He was put to death as a criminal. From first to last, He, the Son of the Eternal, who had become Son of man, was a Man of sorrows, and acquainted with grief. All that He did, all that He suffered—whatever may be our theory of the Atonement—was for our salvation. He was the Good Shepherd, who came to seek and to save the lost sheep, and to die for them. He was the Elder Brother, who came to bring back to their Father the children who had left home and had forgotten Him in the far country.

This has been what the preacher I have quoted might well call 'the traditional and popular theology.' But there is no word about it in the parable. The elder brother in the parable does not give up his wealth and travel to the far country that he may share the miseries of the younger, does not stay with him when the famine comes, does not endure the want, the hunger, the shame. He does nothing, suffers nothing, to recover his younger brother from wretchedness. Instead of this he complains bitterly that his father rejoices over the prodigal's return. Am I, then, to be told that because the glorious gospel of the Church about the Son of God coming to seek and to save the lost is not in the parable, it is false? Am I to be told that the parable must be re-written to get out of it 'the traditional and popular' theory of the coming of Christ to save the world? Am I to be told that because this great gospel of the Son of God being our Elder Brother and coming from heaven to earth to save us is not in the parable, it contradicts the parable, and that, 'no matter how widely it is received and how confidently it is proclaimed, it is not the truth as it is in Jesus'?

Ah, no! the parable is infinitely pathetic and infinitely beautiful. It contains profound discoveries of the mercy and grace which God has shown to mankind. But the parable is an illustration drawn from the life of man. It is a story that might have really happened in a human family. There might have been such a father; there might have been such sons. But no human analogies can comprehend and exhaust the infinite love and the infinite mystery of the relation between the eternal Father and His sinful children. They can but point towards transcendent truths; they can but illustrate,—and at the best illustrate imperfectly,—single aspects of the manifold grace of God.

There is another part of this interpretation of the parable which perhaps, as I am discussing it, it might be just as well to notice before leaving the subject. According to the report, the preacher said, 'There was no word there about satisfying justice before the father could receive the son. The son had borne, and was bearing, the punishment of his own sin, and a substitute was not required, therefore, to satisfy justice, and set free the father's mercy.' And in another part of the sermon the preacher is reported as saying, that 'every sinner bears the punishment of his own sin, and cannot escape.'

Now I do not profess to be able to reconcile these words with other words which occur in the same discourse. Early in the sermon the preacher protests against what he describes as the fashionable theory that nature knows no such thing as the forgiveness of sin, and that we are under the reign of merciless law. He protests against that, but contends that if nature is essentially unforgiving,—if the material universe is not beneficent, or at least making for beneficence,—then we are drifting back on something like the ancient Dualism.

Now that is the line which is commonly taken when the heart is longing to find in nature some clear assurance of the Divine goodness and mercy. But when the Atonement is to be assailed, quite another line is followed. Then we are reminded of the automatic laws of the spiritual world. To quote the words of a very distinguished writer, the ablest and most eminent representative of this school of theological thought: 'These spiritual laws do not need or admit of either vindication, or protection, or support from human or divine hands. Defender or avenger they have none, and they need none. When assailed from any quarter, they avenge themselves, and exact, and continue without fail to exact, so long as the evil remains, the amount of penalty visible and invisible to the veriest jot and tittle which the deed of violation requires.'

This is an explicit and philosophical statement of what I suppose is meant when it is said that 'the prodigal son had borne and was bearing the punishment of his own sin, and a substitute was not required therefore to satisfy justice and set free the father's mercy.' I wonder whether we ought to imagine that the penitent prodigal believed in that theory. I wonder in what words he could have told his father that he believed in it. Perhaps he might have said, 'Father, I have sinned against heaven and against thee, and I do not ask thee to relieve me from any of the just consequences and penalties of my sin. Neither God nor man can relieve me. I have borne, and am still bearing, the punishment of my own sin, and I shall continue to bear it until the penalty is exhausted. I am not worthy to be called thy son. It is part of the just punishment due to me that I should never be treated as a son any more, and that punishment must come upon me; for the punishment is due by the eternal laws to which my conscience bears witness, and by those laws, punishment or reward, visible or invisible, dispenses itself, and in the amount in which either is merited. I am not worthy to be called thy son, and it is impossible that I should ever be called so again.'

That, or something like it, is what the prodigal ought to have said, if every sinner bears the punishment of his own sin and cannot escape it. We must re-write the parable, I am inclined to think, to get that doctrine out of it as well as ours.

But whatever the prodigal may have believed about the impossibility of being released from penalties which he had deserved, and about every man reaping all that he had sown, if he had said that to his father, his father would have swept the miserable theory away as the rising tide sweeps before it the frail structures which children have built upon the sand,—structures which are no unsuitable symbols of these frail theories which human thought has built on the shores of the infinite and eternal mysteries of the Divine love.

'Impossible that I should ever call thee my son again, because thou hast deserved to lose thy place in my heart and in my house, and because every sinner must bear his punishment and cannot escape from it? Impossible? Bring forth quickly the best robe and put it on him, and put a ring on his hand and shoes on his feet, and bring the fatted calf and kill it, and let us eat and drink and be merry. For this my son—listen, *my son*—was dead and is alive again, was lost and is found.' That is better philosophy and better theology than the doctrine which affirms that it is impossible for Christ to bear man's sin, because man, by the eternal necessity of the Divine order, bears all that he deserves.

Which alternative shall we accept? Had the prodigal suffered all that he deserved to suffer? Had he exhausted the just penalties of his wrong-doing when he came home? If he had, it would have been not only ungenerous, but unjust, to refuse him his old place in the family. If he had suffered all he deserved, the place which was his by birth had now come back to him. He had a right to take it again, just as a man who has worked out his term of imprisonment has a legal right to take his place once more among the law-abiding citizens, and to invoke the law in order to protect his freedom. Then what becomes of the father's mercy?

On the other hand, if after all that he had suffered, he still deserved to suffer more, if it was true that he was not worthy to be called his father's son, and could hardly dare to ask to be a hired servant, what then becomes of the assertion that nothing further was required to satisfy justice, and that a sinner cannot escape from the punishment of his sin? The prodigal did escape from a large part of the punishment of his sin, and escaped from it through the father's mercy.

And though there is a deep truth in Paul's declaration that 'whatsoever a man soweth, that shall he also reap,' that declaration does but contain half the truth. We reap what we ourselves sow; but we also reap what Christ sowed; and for eighteen hundred years all Christendom over,—all the world over,—men have been reaping not merely what they have sown themselves, but what Christ sowed for them. And throughout those golden ages which we are hoping for beyond death,—God be thanked,—we are not to reap simply what we ourselves have sown. The great harvest of Christ's righteousness and Christ's love—we are to reap that.

I believe in the remission of sins. If I did not, I should be unfit to preach the Christian gospel, for the gospel assures men of the remission of their sins through Christ. I believe in the remission of the penalties of sin through Christ. Neither you nor I, if we trust in Christ for eternal salvation, are to suffer all that we have deserved for our wrongdoing. Christ has not died in vain; died in vain as the propitiation for the sin of the world. He gave His life for the flock, and the sheep that listen to His voice and follow Him will, through Him, be saved from eternal death.

It is true that the parable contains nothing about the Atonement; but who was it that spoke the parable? Christ is greater than His words, His history greater than His teaching. Why is He here to speak the parable at all? The eternal Son of God—why is He on earth? And why did He, the eternal Son of God, die that awful death on the cross? You may give me a thousand explanations: I prefer His own. 'His blood was shed for the remission of sins.' There is nothing about the Atonement in the parable. No. Human analogies, from which parables are taken, can never represent the infinite love of the Eternal. The father of the parable forgave without effort, without sacrifice. The eternal Father so loved the world that He gave His only begotten Son that He might forgive. There was sacrifice in the eternal love of God when Christ became man—sacrifice immense, immeasurable, on the part of the Father who gave, as well as on the part of the Son who was given. Deny the Atonement,—and you do not increase, you diminish and you dwarf the wonderful and glorious love of God revealed in the Christian redemption.

XIII

THE CENTRAL FACT OF THE GOSPEL

'*I delivered unto you first of all that which I also received, how that Christ died for our sins according to the scriptures.*'—1 COR. xv. 3.

IN the early verses of this chapter, we have an account of the substance of Paul's preaching. This is the Gospel which he preached to the Corinthians, which they had received, and by which, if they held it fast, they were saved. The account is absolutely trustworthy. It is from Paul's own hand, not the hand of another. If we want to learn what he meant when he spoke of the Gospel which is 'the power of God unto salvation,' the authority of these verses is final. He mentions only those truths, those facts, which held the first rank in his preaching, and of these he gives the first place to this—'*Christ died for our sins*.' And this agrees with what he had said earlier in the Epistle: 'The Jews require a sign, and the Greeks seek after wisdom: but we preach Christ';—and not 'Christ' merely, but 'Christ crucified': and Christ is 'the power of God, and the wisdom of God.'

You must have noticed how large a space is given by every one of the Evangelists to the story of our

Lord's last sufferings. And if you think deeply on the agony of Gethsemane, and the terrible and unique circumstances of the conspiracy against His life, His betrayal, His arrest, His crucifixion, and His words on the cross, you will find in them the elements of an awful mystery—a mystery which finds its only sufficient explanation in His declarations—that He laid down His life for His friends, that He gave His life a ransom for many, and that His blood was shed for the remission of sins. The facts contained in the Four Gospels are the root of the doctrine more explicitly set forth in the Epistles: 'He died for us'; 'He was delivered for our trespasses'; 'He suffered for our sins'; 'He died for our sins.' Fact and doctrine are inseparably interlocked. Those parts of our Lord's history which are given in the minutest detail in the Four Gospels contain the great truth that He was the Sacrifice for the sin of the world. This was not the only great truth that Paul preached; but we have it on his own authority that to this he gave the first place.

I find here, therefore, a test of Christian preaching in all churches and in all ages. It is not enough that the truth that Christ died for our sins is formally acknowledged; it must be the central and the supreme fact, and it must be relied upon as the most energetic force in the Christian Gospel. If a preacher gives it a secondary rank, he has somehow missed his way; and the religious life of those who receive a Gospel in which this truth has only a secondary importance will, at the best, be wanting in vigour and depth, in joy and in peace. They will not possess the perfect freedom and the perfect blessedness of the Christian redemption. And of this the experience of nineteen hundred years is a decisive proof.

Place first, for example, the ethical perfection to which Christ calls us, and whatever admiration that fair vision may excite, there will be no power to achieve it. Place first the great truth of Divine Fatherhood, and whatever transcendent passion and enthusiasm it may inspire, there will be no clear, enduring, vivid consciousness that we are the children of the Eternal. Place first the great discovery of immortal righteousness and immortal joy to which God has destined us in Christ, and the glorious hope, though it may kindle the imagination, will have no firm hold upon the heart, and will exert no sovereign authority over conduct. Place first the great gift of inspiration assured to all Christian men and women through all time, and though there may be dazzling forms of religious experience, ambitious strivings after union with God, occasional and surprising intuitions of the Divine glory, life and character will not be transfigured by the indwelling of the Holy Ghost. Does any preacher give the first and central place in the Christian Gospel to any other truth—no matter how noble that truth may be—he is preaching what Paul would have called 'another Gospel'—a Gospel of his own, not the Gospel which those who stand in the true succession have received from God and the first preachers of the Christian faith.

This subject might be treated speculatively, but I propose this morning to treat it under some of its practical aspects.

'*First of all—Christ died for our sins.*' Any conception of the death of Christ that makes this remarkable form of expression unnatural—any explanation of it which practically explains it away—impairs the whole structure of the Christian faith and weakens the central forces of the Christian life. It is true, no doubt, that the Christian Gospel may be partially received while the intellect and the heart resent—and it is generally the heart rather than the intellect which resents—this great fact. Christ may be known in a vague and imperfect manner as the Saviour of men, and there may be genuine trust in Him for eternal salvation, while the truth that He died for our sins is misconceived, rejected, or evaded; but sooner or later we must come to it. We must come to it, if we are to know that Gospel which met in deadly conflict the heathenism of the ancient world and mastered it, subdued the power of Rome, converted and civilised the fierce races which laid the foundations of modern Europe, gave fortitude to martyrs, inspired with courage and zeal the leaders of the great revivals of faith in more recent ages, and the great reformers of apostate churches. Sooner or later we must come to it, if the Christian Gospel is to be in our hands the power of God unto the salvation of our people at home and the countless millions of heathen abroad. Sooner or later we must come to it, if we ourselves are to enter into the fulness of the Christian redemption.

You may say, perhaps, that this truth may surely be dismissed because it is so mysterious. Is it not the insoluble problem of theology? Is not the theory of it inaccessible to human thought? But I am speaking not of Christian theology, but of the Christian Gospel—not of the explanation and philosophy of the Atonement, but of the fact. '*Christ died for our sins*': that is very mysterious, no doubt. But is that a reason why we should not insist upon it? This is what Paul preached,—not to people like yourselves, who have been educated from childhood in the Christian faith, who are familiar with the story of Christ and the contents of the Christian Scriptures, who inherit the traditions of sixty generations of Christian thought and life,—but to heathen men at Corinth; and they received it, they stood fast in it, and by it Paul says they were saved. If it was within their grasp, it ought not to be beyond yours.

'*Christ died for our sins*': for our sins. That places Christ apart from every other religious teacher that ever lived. Who else has died—or could die—for your sins and mine? It places the death of Christ apart from every other death in the history of the world, and brings it into a close, wonderful, awful relation to each one of us and to all that is worst in each one of us, to all that is most truly our own in each one of us, to all that should shame, and humble, and distress us the most. If, therefore, we want to deal fairly with the Christian Gospel as Paul preached it, we must begin with our sins and with the fact that Christ died for our sins. Many of us, perhaps, have evaded, and are evading still, this clear and obvious duty. I find that men prefer to think of many other things first; they want to find God, and ask Christ how they are to find Him. Or they want to know in what relations they and other men stand to God, and are very curious about the eternal destiny of other men as well as their own. Or, dismissing their sins and the fact that Christ died for them, men want to become better; and they read the words of Christ to discover the true laws of conduct, and how they are to become strong enough to obey them. Or they are in trouble, and they turn to Christ for consolation. Now, we may come to Christ for all these things, and should go to Him for all these things; but Paul tells us that when he was dealing with the Corinthians he insisted that first of all they should consider and learn that Christ died for our sins.

Our *sins.* Paul is not speaking of crimes merely, or of vices merely, or of grave moral faults, though all these are sins. Many men are criminals because, having been born under very hard conditions, or exposed, in later years, to very fierce temptations, the sin that is in them has taken a form which society is obliged to punish for the sake of protecting life, and property, and public order. Men's moral character depends very much on temperament. The sin which is in some men naturally breaks out into brutal outrages or into gross sensual excesses. That is partly a matter of physical constitution. Some men are so made that in them sin could not take these flagrant forms. Then, again, moral character is largely determined by environment and education. Many of us have been so disciplined that the sin which is in us has been prevented from appearing in any of the grosser vices; we are truthful, just, industrious, and temperate largely because of the conditions under which we were born and under which we were disciplined in early youth. In other men there has been no such moral discipline, and their sin has been left free to show itself in lying, indolence, dishonesty, intemperance, and still fouler vices.

Moral conduct and moral character are, I say, in part—and largely—the result of temperament, or what we call a man's natural constitution; in part—and largely—the result of those complex conditions and influences which contributed to the development of his physical, intellectual, and moral life in childhood and youth; in part—and largely—the result of the circumstances of his maturer years. In part, I say, and largely—not altogether. There are vices from which a man is saved by his temperament; but it is for him to choose whether he will be guilty of the vices to which his temperament makes him liable. There are grave faults, the very seeds of which seem to be destroyed by early education; but each man has to determine whether he will check and subdue the growth of other faults—perhaps not less grave—against which his early education has not protected him. There are some moral offences to which some men are not tempted; their circumstances give no provocation—perhaps no opportunity—to commit them; the virtue of such men is tried by solicitations to other forms of moral evil. The immense influence of natural constitution, of education, of environment on moral character is incontestable, but it is not omnipotent. At the very centre of the life of every man, surrounded by those provinces of his nature over which forces that he can resist but cannot command exert a powerful control—at the very centre of the life of every man there is the man's inner self,—his will. Fate and freedom—not fate alone, not freedom alone, but fate and freedom together—determine conduct and determine destiny.

And the supreme question for each one of us is the relation of that inner self—the centre of our life—to the living God. Attribute as much importance as you like to the influence on your moral character of physical constitution, early training or want of training, the temper of your friends, the conditions of your common occupation, the anxieties and cares and claims of business, the moral atmosphere you are compelled to breathe—attribute as much as you like to the influence of all these things, but you must come at last to the vital question,—What is your own relation,—the relation of your true and real self,—to God? That lies in your own hands.

Have you been kept from evil, or really and powerfully induced to resist evil even when the resistance has been unsuccessful, by the dread of God's displeasure? Have you endeavoured to do right, even when the endeavour has failed, in order to win God's approval? Have you, in a word, accepted Him with reverence and awe and yet with perfect joy as your God, confessing His sovereign authority over your personal life, His absolute claims to your obedience, your worship, your faith, your love? Has it become clear to you that because of His august, His glorious righteousness, His infinite grace, your perfection and your blessedness are to be achieved by the practical acknowledgment of these claims in this world and in the unknown worlds beyond death? Has every natural or acquired virtue, when assaulted by temptation, received support from your reverence for His supreme Will? And when the strength of virtue has begun to fail, has this reverence for Him been an effective force in prolonging the struggle? Has it sometimes—has it often—given you the victory? When you have been called to duties which were unfamiliar, unwelcome, and which were alien from your natural temper, has your loyalty to Him been motive enough to induce you to attempt the righteousness which but for Him you would have left altogether unattempted?

The Christian Gospel—which begins with the

declaration that Christ died for our sins—assumes that this inner self of ours—this true self—is impatient of Divine control; it assumes that whatever our moral character may be, we resist or forget the Divine authority,—and that is sin. It assumes that the august sovereignty of the living personal God is rejected in that central region of life which determines what a man really is and what his destiny must be. We recognise—many of us—the claims of duty, but we resist the personal authority of God; and that is what is meant by sin. To put it in another way, the Christian Gospel assumes that every man is a sinner. The assumption is not merely that in every man there are faults of character and faults of conduct which may be attributed in part, at least, to his physical constitution, for which he is not responsible, or to his education and circumstances, for which he is not responsible, but that in the man's real self—in the very centre of his life, there is an indisposition—a settled refusal—to place the perfectly righteous will of God above his own will, and to acknowledge with affectionate reverence God's august authority. Is that assumption true? Each man can answer for himself. Here is a point at which we can judge whether Christ knows us as He knows the Father.

Will you consider it? Here is something which the Christian Gospel declares about ourselves. Whether you have considered it before or not, will you consider it, and consider it seriously, and consider it soon? Do not be satisfied with dismissing it either with an impatient denial, or an evasion, or a half-hearted acknowledgment of its truth. The first time you have an hour's quiet, your mind being active and keen, descend into the depths of your personal life; find yourself; remember that the living God is near, searching you through and through; follow the search with Him; ask yourself, with a serious, relentless desire to know the truth, whether in your real, innermost self you have habitually and effectually acknowledged Him as your God. Do not ask whether, under some strong impulse coming upon you from without, you have felt awe and reverence for His greatness and have been thrilled with delight by His infinite love. Do not ask whether, under some mysterious impulse which may have had its springs in the eternal life of God Himself, you have sometimes been agitated with deep religious emotion, with a passion of penitence or of gratitude, or with the desire for perfect righteousness. The impulse from without soon spends its force. The gracious, mysterious influence comes and goes. Impulse and influence alike have their origin elsewhere—not in yourself; they do not reveal, except in the way you respond to them, the central element of your own life. How has it been—how is it, between you—you yourself—and God? Face that question. It is clearly the ultimate question for all of us; and if you are at last constrained to acknowledge that you have not made Him the end of your life, the law of your life, the root of your life, the joy of your life, go on to consider the seriousness of the acknowledgment and all that it involves—the guilt of it and the peril of it. You may then pass to your personal habits, your temper or disposition, your practical aims, and ask what difference it would have made if you, in your inner self, your true self, had been always loyal to God, —if He had had His right place in your system of life.

And it may be well to single out some special defect or fault of which you are conscious—some grave offence of which you have been guilty, perhaps only once or only twice in your history. You have not thought it a very serious thing; it has left your general character, as you think, unaffected; it has been too occasional to be fatal. But follow the suggestion which I once met with: suppose that Christ had had this fault, or had committed only occasionally, only once, this grave offence—would it not have quenched the glory of the world? That solitary fault, that one offence,—would it not have impoverished the moral and spiritual life of mankind? Do you think now that the fault, the offence, is not a very serious thing? Do you think now that it is not fatal? Or if you think a single fault unimportant, a single offence not fatal, the true method to try the trustworthiness of your judgment is in imagination to attribute that single fault to One who had no other, or to suppose the offence committed by One who, but for that, would have been absolutely free from sin. And then, in imagination,—if you want to try and test the real character of your own offences,—add to the life and history of our Lord fault after fault of which you are conscious, and which you deplore, offence after offence which you have regretted, but which you have repeated; and then tell me whether these sins are not appalling, and whether they ought not to fill us with shame and with alarm.

Christ *died* for our sins—for those sins which, according to the Christian Gospel, we have all committed.

Yes, you believe that He died for our sins,—and some of you explain it by adding that He died to reveal the love of God to us, and to touch our hearts and to draw us to a better and a devouter life; and you are very anxious sometimes to receive the full force of this revelation of God's love, and to be conscious that you are being delivered by it from moral evil. No doubt these are among the ultimate effects of the Death of Christ; but do not push aside Paul's words. What you say—and Paul could have said it if he had meant it—is that Christ died to inspire us with trust in God and love for God, and to make us righteous men and women. That is true; but what Paul says here is something else—he says that Christ died for our *sins*—died because of our want of trust in God and our want of love for Him—died because of our unrighteousness. Try to meet that declaration, not to evade it. When we discover that we have been in the wrong there is something so humiliating in it, and, if we continue to think of it, so distressing, that we are impatient to get right. We are in haste to dismiss the evil past—the evil that still infects the present; and when we hear of the great redemption that is in Christ, we spring at it and ask for power to live righteously. We think that this should be our only solicitude; we think that to give us this was the only object of the life and death and resurrection of our Lord.

Paul says: No. Our sins are too serious to be dealt with in this way. First of all—among the chief contents of the Christian Gospel—is this: Christ died for our sins—*died* for them.

This has to be faced. It is humiliating. It is awful. Christ, the Eternal Son of God, became man, and died for the sins of men. This is the meaning of the agony of Gethsemane, when it may almost be said that He began to die. This is the meaning of His surrender to the guard that came to arrest Him, when He might have smitten them to the ground and have escaped. This is the meaning of His physical sufferings on the cross. This is the meaning of His desolate cry, 'My God! My God! why hast Thou forsaken Me?' '*I delivered unto you first of all*' —listen! the Apostle speaks to us as he spoke to the Corinthians—'*I delivered unto you first of all, that Christ died for our sins.*'

As I have asked you to descend into the depths of your moral life, and to verify for yourselves the assumption of the Gospel that we have all sinned, I ask you also in solitary hours to dwell upon this wonderful fact—that Christ died for your sins—for yours—and to dwell on it until it is rooted in your intellect and your heart for ever. Take our Lord's account of it as well as Paul's. His blood was shed for the remission of sins. Hold firmly to the fact—put aside all explanations that conceal or deny it. Take the fact as Paul states it, as Christ states it. Neither Paul nor Christ says that this awful death was to touch the heart of God to mercy, and to move Him to pity us. God loves saint and sinner alike; He so loved the world that He gave His only-begotten Son; the love was the origin and the cause of the Coming and Death of Christ, not the effect of it. But the awful thing about our sin is that, though God loves us, the remission of our sins—the forgiveness which we regard as a matter of course—is declared to be the result of the Death of Christ; and I suppose, apart from that Death, it would have been impossible.

I have not attempted to offer any explanation of this great central fact of the Christian Gospel,—not because I suppose that here and there we may not discover light in the darkness of this great mystery. But it is possible for men to be embarrassed when they attempt to receive the fact, because at the same time they attempt to receive some inadequate explanation of it. The fact may be rejected because the explanation may be intolerable. But in all other departments of thought we begin with the fact and stand fast to the fact, though one theory after another that is offered in illustration of it is apparently unsatisfactory. And this fact, that Christ died for our sins, is part of the Christian Gospel—is wrought into the substance of apostolic life and teaching—is wrought into the substance of the very story of Christ's life and death. It holds its place among the primary, the regal truths of the Christian revelation. It is part of the strong foundation of our faith in God; it is the root of our immortal hope. In all the great days of the Church its greatness has been acknowledged with a passionate devotion. It is not a speculation—it is necessary to the perfection of Christian life and strength, to the joy of worship, to the blessedness of communion with the Father. It is the last and supremest guarantee of our kinship with the Eternal Son of God. He is so intimately one with us, that on Him the burden of the world's sin could rest, and because of His confession of it, and His endurance of death for it, the sin could be forgiven. It is the glorious assurance of the Divine Fatherhood. It kindles the fires of an infinite love for Christ. It fills the heart at once with compassion and with hope in the presence of the sins of mankind. And those who have received most deeply into their very life the discovery of God's relationship to them in the Death of Christ have had their hearts filled with the most passionate joy in the Divine love, with the deepest and intensest faith in the compassions which fail not, and the mercy which endureth for ever.

XIV

PERFECT SALVATION

'*Wherein ye greatly rejoice, though now for a little while, if need be, ye have been put to grief in manifold temptations, that the proof of your faith, being more precious than gold that perisheth though it is proved by fire, might be found unto praise and glory and honour at the revelation of Jesus Christ.*'—1 PETER i. 6, 7.

THESE words have reminded me of a phrase which, twenty or thirty years ago, was constantly recurring in sermons of many of the younger and more ardent preachers of that time. They insisted that Christ had come to achieve for us what they described as a *present salvation*. I daresay many of you can remember a time when very earnest men were always using that phrase, and those who used it spoke of the *present salvation* with passion and enthusiasm, as men to whom a great discovery had come, —a discovery which might add immensely to the spiritual force and blessedness of all who received it. There was a polemical element, too, in preaching of this kind, for the doctrine of a *present salvation* was asserted as though it were a part of the Christian Gospel that had never been clearly apprehended, or that had been forgotten. It was implied that most Christian people had thought of salvation as something future, something remote, something that could not be known on this side of death: while in fact we are to be saved, if saved at all, here and now. I suppose that to very many this preaching of a present salvation was, for a time at least, very animating. It lifted life to new heights; it gave new faith and new courage; it brought the Christian redemption very near, and made it very real.

I have said that there was a polemical element in this teaching. It was an attack—open or implied—on modes of Christian thought, by which it was supposed that the Christian life had been impaired and enfeebled. The attack was sometimes open and resolute. Those who preached a present salvation said in substance,—'Many of you Christian people have missed the power and glory which Christ came to make yours in this life, because you are always thinking of heaven and the life to come: your religion is unpractical; you do not see that Christ came to make an infinite difference in the whole life of man in this world, as well as to make eternal blessedness our inheritance in the next.' There is no need to preach like that now. None of us, I imagine, are too much occupied with thoughts of heaven and the life to come. Richard Baxter, as some of you remember, tells us that in the afternoon, when it began to be too dark to go on with his reading and writing, and before the candles were brought in, he used to sit quietly in the twilight meditating on the Saints' Everlasting Rest. There are not many Christian people, I imagine, who spend much of their time in that way now.

The polemic element of the preaching about the present salvation, the attack on dwelling too much upon the future blessedness of the righteous,—this, whether by its own vigour, or, perhaps, by the action of many powerful influences allied with it, has been very successful. Whether the positive element—which is gloriously true—has been equally effective, I cannot tell. I mean that we do not know whether generally God is nearer to us in this life than He was to our fathers; whether we have now and here more of that Divine peace which is untroubled by the vicissitudes of human life; whether the eternal Kingdom to which we already belong, exerts a more effective control over us, makes us more indifferent than our fathers were to the accumulation of wealth, to the enjoyment of the inferior pleasures of this transient life, to human opinion and to all the powers of this visible order. I do not know whether we have a firmer strength for doing the will of God, or a deeper consciousness of the infinite difference it makes to us in this life whether or not we are in Christ. Whether we realise the present salvation more fully than our fathers did, I cannot tell: it is certain, I imagine, that we think very much less about any salvation that is still to come.

There is a glorious truth, as I have said, in this teaching about a present salvation,—but not all the truth. It is even possible that those who thought so much more about the life to come than we think, may have had a larger measure of God's power with them in this life. I express no judgment. It may have been so.

Whenever any truth that has not had an adequate place in the thought and life of the Church breaks through the clouds and fills the minds and hearts of any number of Christian people with its light and glory, they seem to think that until that hour the whole Church had been living in darkness because this truth had been forgotten; they speak as if no other truth had been remembered. Everything had been wrong—because on this point the Church had not been right. And that is presumption; that is spiritual conceit. The line of saints has never been broken. The promise has been fulfilled—'Where two or three are gathered together in My name, there am I in the midst of them.' And where Christ is, everything cannot be in ruins. The promise has been fulfilled that the Holy Spirit should be with the Church for ever; and where the Holy Spirit is, there must be light, however heavy the clouds may be. The right method surely, when we think that a forgotten truth has, through God's infinite goodness, come to us, is to ask—how it came to be forgotten; and if those who insisted so much on the present salvation had asked that question, they might have come to the conclusion that the greatness and glory of the present salvation had not been sufficiently thought of because the Church, in times of great spiritual earnestness and clear spiritual vision, had seen that there is a salvation still to come greater and more glorious. And then, instead of discouraging the hope of that larger redemption, they would have said to their brethren: 'Still continue to look forward with eager hope and with great joy to the blessedness and perfection of the life to come, but rejoice, too, that already you have received the remission of sins and the eternal life, are the sons of God, the brethren of Christ, and that the Spirit of God dwells in you.' There is a present salvation, there is also a salvation to be hoped for.

'*Wherein ye greatly rejoice.*' The words refer, I think, to the whole of the contents of the preceding verses. We are to rejoice that 'the God and Father of our Lord Jesus Christ, according to His great mercy, begat us again unto a living hope by the resurrection of Jesus Christ from the dead.' That is—the resurrection of Christ is an event—the greatest of all events—in our own personal history. When He rose from the dead, human life ascended to a higher level, became greater than it was before, was detached and disentangled from powers which repressed and restricted its true energies, was completely penetrated with the love of God, and entered completely into God's eternal kingdom. And Christ—not the earthly Christ but the ascended and glorified Christ—is the Head of the new race. His larger, diviner human life is ours. And the life which we have received from Him, and into the full possession of which He entered at His Resurrection and Ascension,—that life has in its essence the hope and assurance of passing into the same glory into which Christ has entered. For this visible and earthly order is not its home; it belongs to the invisible and the eternal; it will breathe at last its native air, and see bending over it the splendours of its native skies. Having this life we are born, therefore, to 'an inheritance incorruptible, and undefiled, and that fadeth not away,'—an eternal inheritance, an inheritance that can never be profaned and defiled by the invasion of the enemies of God and of righteousness, whose flowers will never wither, whose fertility will never be desolated. This inheritance is not here; it is not ours in possession yet—the possession of it is no part of the present salvation; it is reserved for us in heaven. And lest we should come to harm before we reach it, we are guarded by the power of God through faith, and so kept safely for the salvation which is '*ready to be revealed in the last time*.'

In this it is that we Christian people are to rejoice. The *present* salvation is an incomplete salvation; the *perfect* salvation is to come.

The future life of those who are to live for ever in God—the complete salvation—transcends all thought as well as all hope; we cannot see the inheritance for the golden haze that surrounds it; it is too intensely bright for mortal vision; it belongs to another order than this, which has conditioned the development of all our powers; it cannot be revealed to knowledge until it is revealed in experience. But some elements of the present salvation will in the future salvation be perfect. Our sins, through the infinite mercy of God, through Him who is the Propitiation for our sins, and not for ours only, but also for the sins of the whole world—our sins are already forgiven, and we may have the full assurance that they are forgiven. To those who have had any deep sense of the evil of sin, who have felt in their very heart that it is an awful thing, a thing of horror, damnable,—forgiveness is very wonderful; and the consciousness that there is peace between us and the Eternal, the energy of whose infinite life is hostile to sin, brings with it a certain awe as well as a great blessedness.

But not until we are capable of a clearer and fuller knowledge of God, not until our life at every point, instead of at a single point, touches the infinite life of God—not till then shall we ever know the infinite blessedness of the discovery that as far as the East is from the West, so far hath He removed our transgressions from us, that He has blotted out our sins as a thick cloud which vanishes and leaves no stain on the blue of heaven. That blessedness is to come.

There are times when the manifestations of the love of God for us—the present manifestations of the love of the living God—manifestations given to us in secret and wonderful ways by the power of the Spirit of God,—make the heart tremble with a blended reverence and joy. We have no strength to bear them for long. If they remained, glory would break upon glory, and we should anticipate the blessedness we hope for. But they cannot remain; the glory passes and the common light of day returns, though that, too, is touched for ever with a new splendour which cannot wholly fade away. What we hope for,—what we know we shall inherit,—is a life with powers so enlarged and so invigorated, and with so Divine an environment, that these manifestations of the personal love of the Eternal for us, and manifestations still more wonderful, will be with us always; that we shall move freely among them as we move in the common air and in the light of the common sun; that they will never become dim, never be interrupted, but that in their tenderness and in their power they will increase through age after age of increasing wonder and increasing joy. When God has His children with Him, oh, how wonderful will the revelations of His love for them become!

Here—in the power of the life which has its roots in Christ and receives its inspiration from the Holy Spirit—we may achieve righteousness and saintliness. I do not care, for my own part, to contest the faith of those who insist that some have actually reached what they describe as Christian perfection—or complete consecration—a condition in which the will never swerves from its loyalty to God, never consents to thought or act that is known to be sinful, never refuses to meet the obligations of any recognised duty. It may be so; who can tell—but God? But it would be too large a claim—it would be a claim impossible to concede—if it were further contended that here any man ever has an infallible perception of what is sinful and a complete knowledge of duty. The trouble is, for many of us at least, that we do not discover the sinfulness till we have sinned; we do not recognise the duty till the time has passed for discharging it. And if, happily, in any man the will is true and faithful, and if it is always alert and vigilant, there are large regions of our nature in which there are powers of evil which are always struggling into revolt, even though they may be subdued—powers which, though crucified and dying, are not dead. The true self of every man—while it may have its centre and root in the divine life—is implicated and involved in a baser life which is hostile to the divine; and so the present salvation is incomplete.

But the day of liberation will come, when, in the clear light of God, we shall know perfectly the perfect life, and shall never, through a false judgment, mistake the will of the Eternal; when every spontaneous impulse will be the ally of conscience; when the strong currents of emotion and passion will flow in one channel and carry us swiftly to new and nobler ideals of righteousness; when every devout purpose will be equalled or transcended by achievement; when our better self will be disengaged from the flesh, and will receive—or, in the power of God, create for itself—an organism through which, without painful effort, it will be able to accomplish all His will; when all the external conditions of life will be sacraments and channels of grace; and when in the unbroken fellowship with saints and with God we shall be animated and enabled to rise through age after age to loftier heights of perfection and of joy. And so in every element of the present salvation we may discover the promise of a larger salvation to come.

There is something in this great hope to give us courage and to renew the strength which too often faints and the resolution which too often falters. We do unwisely, I venture to think, to dispense with the energy which we may derive from the blessed and perfect future. The joy of the Christian life would be immeasurably augmented if we dwelt more constantly on its eternal consummation in the Divine-Presence, and the joy would give strength. We have great memories to sustain us,—and, above all, the memory of the supreme manifestation of the Divine love in the life and death and resurrection of Jesus Christ. But when Hope is confederate with Memory, and both are confirmed by the present consciousness that we have found God, every power of our better life receives new animation, and we see that all things are possible to us.

Further—apart from a clear vision of the perfect salvation—faith is subject to an unnecessary strain. Forget to how large and free and blessed a life men are destined in Christ in the next world, and it will sometimes seem as if there were a disproportion between the great discoveries of the Christian Gospel and what the Gospel has actually accomplished. The Incarnation and the Death of Christ; the descent of the Eternal Son of God from inaccessible heights of glory to the limitations of human life, to pain, to unknown depths of darkness; the sorrows through which He passed when He became the Sacrifice for the sin of the world—surely something more should come of all these than the imperfect righteousness which is achieved in this world by those whom He saves—the peace so often broken,—the joy so often clouded,—the vision of God, which at its strongest and clearest is so dim. Does that which we see and know and experience already exhaust the power of that august Divine humiliation and the purposes of that infinite Divine love? The results—if we see them all—were they worth the cost?

It is as if you were to judge of the worth of labour which has been spent upon the fields by their appearance in early spring, when the dark ground is hardly relieved by the faint green of the wheat which has just begun to shoot—it is so frail, apparently of so little value. Is this all that is to come of cleaning the ground and ploughing it and enriching it for the seed? You must wait—wait till the spring has expanded into the bright days of summer, and the summer into early autumn; and then the corn ripened, perfected, rising and falling in golden billows under the glowing sun, will reveal the end for which the farmer laboured. And Christ's harvest time is not here, but in worlds unseen. Not until we know the perfect righteousness and the perfect blessedness of the saints in glory shall we see for what great ends the Son of God became man, and suffered, and died, and rose again.

In the presence of the struggle, prolonged through so many ages, of the eternal righteousness of God with the sin of our race, and its doubtful triumphs—in the presence of the baffled mercy of God, which even in the Church achieves for men so incomplete a salvation, Faith may falter and be troubled. For its vigour—for its rapture, it needs the inspiration and support of the great hope of the complete salvation which is ready to be revealed in the last time. If the present salvation had been forgotten, those did well who reminded us of its greatness; but to forget the salvation which is hereafter to be revealed is to impoverish the wealth, and almost to paralyse the power, of the salvation that God grants us in this present life.

XV

SAVING TRUTH[1]

'*The gospel which I preached unto you, which also ye received, wherein also ye stand, by which also ye are saved.*'—1 COR. xv. 1.

'THE Gospel which I preached unto you . . . by which also ye are *saved*.' The words recall a phrase which was in very common use among all Evangelical Christians forty or fifty years ago, but which is now rarely heard among Congregationalists and is almost forgotten. Our fathers used to talk about *saving truth*—truth which has saving power in it—truth which the Church has to make known to all men and to persuade them to receive in order that they may be saved. It has ceased, I think, to be our habit to speak of truth in that way. Were our fathers in the right when they spoke of *saving truth*—or were they in the wrong?

The old phrase has not disappeared by accident; or simply because the sharp outlines of the thought

[1] This sermon was preached to my own congregation on Sunday morning, December 4th, 1892. It was preached again a few months later, with considerable additions suggested by the occasion, in Allen Street Chapel, Kensington, at one of the services held in celebration of the centenary of the Congregational Church assembling in that building.—R. W. D.

which had been impressed upon it had been worn down so that it had lost its meaning. I can remember when there were definite and earnest protests against it. There were some who said—What a man believes can be of no great and critical importance either in this world or the next; it is not his belief that saves a man or ruins him, but his conduct. There were others who took a different line. Men are saved—so some of us contended—not by Truth but by the grace of God through Christ; if salvation consists in the forgiveness of sin, it is not Truth that forgives us but God Himself: nor are we forgiven for the sake of Truth but for Christ's sake; if salvation consists in righteous and holy living, it is in the power of the life which God has given us in Christ, and in the power of the Holy Spirit—not in the power of Truth—that righteousness and holiness are possible to us. And so the old phrase—*saving truth*—got a bad name, and was driven out of use. I wonder whether it has ever been heard in this pulpit during the last thirty years.

There was real cause, I think, for the hostility which the phrase provoked. For the belief of certain truths—and of certain truths which were commonly stated in the form of abstract propositions, defining what has been achieved for us in the Christian redemption—was sometimes described as if it were the decisive act by which men pass out of darkness into the light of God. Some of us, perhaps, whose religious life began in those distant years, can remember how anxious we were to be quite sure—first, that we had right conceptions of these regal truths, and next, that our belief in them was of the right kind. For a time we were clear that the deep cravings of our heart for the assurance of the divine forgiveness and for the consciousness that we had received the divine life were not satisfied. We had no happy sense that we had come home to God. No new freedom had come to us ; no new power. And we supposed that the reason must be that our conception of the saving truths was not accurate, and we endeavoured to discover exactly where our error was ; or else we supposed that our belief was not the right sort of belief, or that it was not strong and firm enough. For weeks, for months, perhaps for years, we were so occupied with certain great doctrines about Christ that we never came near to Christ Himself. When we learnt that it was Christ—not merely the truth about Christ—that was to save us, it seemed a new Gospel. We turned from the truth to Him and were saved. The Christian men to whose teaching we listened never intended that our supreme concern should be about truth, and that we should remain at a distance from Christ for so long ; but I think that their way of speaking about '*saving truth*' led large numbers of people—and not unnaturally—into this error. And so, as I have said, the old phrase '*saving truth*' got a bad name, and was driven out of use.

Then followed one of a thousand illustrations of our inability to reject one error without falling into another. Truth—truth by itself—men said, cannot save us; and therefore they argued that Truth has nothing to do with our salvation. This was an error which was hardly less fatal than the one which they rejected. They were wholly in the right when they discovered—if it was a discovery—that Truth by itself cannot save us; they were wholly in the wrong when they failed to see that Truth is one of the great forces by which God saves us.

If a man asks me whether he is guilty of sin because he is unable to receive some of the great truths of the Christian Gospel, I cannot answer him. Who but God can tell whether his inability to receive them arises from intellectual causes, for which he is irresponsible, or from moral causes, for which he is responsible? Who but God can tell whether it arises from the defective manner in which the truths have been presented to him? But though his inability may imply no moral or religious fault, it involves him in the gravest moral and religious loss. Whether a man is to be condemned for not receiving certain great Christian truths is a question which only God can determine, because God alone knows why he does not receive them. But that in rejecting them he rejects certain great forces in the power of which he might live a Christian life is certain.

You remember the parable of the sower. Christ compares the word to seed, and describes the seed as revealing its power in conduct and character. Where His Word is not understood,—that is, where the Truth which the Word stands for is not understood—and where it is not held fast, it is like seed which is carried off by the birds; nothing comes of it; there is no crop. That is a precisely accurate description of large numbers of persons who read the Bible and listen to sermons. They are soothed or they are excited; they have the feeling that it is good to read and good to listen; but they understand hardly anything that they read or hear, and they retain less. Ask them what our Lord meant when He spoke to Nicodemus about the necessity of being born again; or when He said to the woman at the well that the water which He gives to a man 'shall become in him a well of water springing up unto eternal life'; or when He said to the disciples that 'no one knoweth who the Son is save the Father; and who the Father is, save the Son, and he to whomsoever the Son willeth to reveal Him': or ask them what Paul meant when he spoke of our being 'justified by faith'; of there being 'no condemnation to them that are in Christ Jesus'; or of our being 'not in the flesh but in the spirit, if so be that the Spirit of God dwelleth' in us;—and you will find that they have no real knowledge of the truths for which the words stand. Or if, when you remind them of the words, they are able to attach some vague meaning to them, it is obvious that the meaning has never been firmly grasped, and is not resolutely held. The divine seed has been carried off by the birds, and they are none the better for it. In contrast with these, our Lord places those who, having heard the word of God, understand it, hold it fast, and bring forth fruit, some a hundredfold, some sixty, some thirty. The Truth contained in the divine Word is to Christian life and character what the seed is to the plant. If Truth by itself cannot save us, it has clearly a great deal to do with saving us.

Passage after passage to the same effect might be quoted from the Old Testament and the New, from our Lord's discourses, from the ancient Psalms, from the apostolic Epistles. You remember Paul's words in his Epistle to the Romans: 'I am not ashamed of the Gospel: for it is the power of God unto salvation to every one that believeth.' Mark those words:—the *Gospel* is the power of God unto salvation; the *Gospel*. If, therefore, we ministers fail to make clear to men the contents of the Gospel, or if they refuse to believe the Gospel, this 'power of God' becomes, as far as those to whom we speak are concerned, ineffective. The words of Paul in the text are also very much to the purpose: 'I make known unto you, brethren, the Gospel which I preached unto you, which also ye received, wherein also ye stand, by which also *ye are saved*.' When our fathers spoke of '*saving truth*' they were not far wrong after all.

I

Shall we try to discover how the Gospel saves us? I do not propose to travel over the whole of the immense region which this inquiry opens to us. I shall omit to notice altogether some of the most important considerations which the inquiry suggests. For I do not want to deliver a theological lecture: I want to deal with the subject in as practical a way as I am able.

We must look first at the account of the Gospel which Paul gives in this chapter. It is a brief account; a very simple account: elsewhere he speaks of truths contained in it which here are not explicitly mentioned. In this chapter he states what things they were that held the first place in the Gospel which he preached to the Corinthians; and they are these:—'Christ died for our sins according to the Scriptures: He was buried: He hath been raised on the third day according to the Scriptures'; and then Paul recalls certain remarkable appearances of Christ to His disciples after His resurrection. He says that it is by believing these things, holding fast to these things, that the Corinthians are to be saved; believing in Christ's death for the sins of men; Christ's Burial; Christ's Resurrection; and believing that the Death, Burial, and Resurrection were not mere accidents, but were the fulfilment of God's gracious purposes; that they were 'according to the Scriptures.' How does belief in this Gospel save us? As I have said, I do not propose to deliver a theological lecture. I want to approach the question by lines of thought along which you will be most likely to travel with me. I want to deal with it from the side of common human experience.

(1) Will you then consider and explain to mê what would save you from habits of thought, habits of speech, habits of conduct for which you condemn yourself, but which you cannot break? There have been men who regarded sin—their own sin—with horror, disgust, and hatred; men who passed through an agony of suffering if they had given place even for a few minutes to impure thoughts; men who, if they had been betrayed into false or even ungenerous words—or into actions which were unkind or unjust, were tortured as by the touch of fire; men to whom the shame of having felt secret resentment against God, or secret distrust of His goodness, was as distressing as the shame of other men when they had been guilty of a baseness or cruelty which had called down upon them public execration. Do you think that if you felt any of this deep abhorrence and dread of sin your life would have a higher quality? Are you sometimes distressed that sin should give you such little distress? Is it clear to you that until you have an habitual dread of sinning, and until you shrink from it as you shrink from physical pain, you are likely to continue to sin?

Have you thought about the evil of sin with the hope of kindling in your heart the fires of a fierce and enduring hatred of it; and have the fires refused to burn, or have they soon gone down? Have you prayed to God to enable you to hate sin, and prayed in vain?

Listen to Paul's Gospel—Christ died for our sins.

That is the power of God unto the salvation of every man who believes it; it saves a man from his indifference and insensibility to the enormous evil of failing to love and obey God, and failing to love and serve mankind. Christ—the Son of God—think of it—Christ through whom all things were made—Christ the Son of God in whom all things in Heaven and Earth consist—died for the sins of men. To millions upon millions of men this has made sin most hateful and most appalling. Believe it,—really believe it,—and the experience of sixty generations assures us that through God's grace it will make sin most hateful and most appalling to *you*. I do not ask you to construct a theory of it; the theory is no part of the Gospel itself, though to every active mind that receives the truth some theory will be necessary; but it is the fact on which we must dwell—Christ the Eternal Son of God died for our sins,—died that we might receive remission of sins. It is God's own demonstration of the appalling evil of sin. It is a '*saving truth*.'

(2) Let me ask again—Do you think that duty would be discharged more cheerfully, that temptation would be resisted more firmly, that trouble would be endured with greater patience and courage, that the passion for wealth and mastery would be cooled, and every generous and divine affection made more fervent and intense, if the Lord Jesus Christ had the supreme place in your life;—if, as soon as you woke in the morning, your heart leapt with joy

because you remembered that He is near;—if during the day—in solitude, and when crowds of men were round you—the light of His presence broke again and again through the clouds of earthly anxiety and care, and if again and again you heard His gracious voice rising above the tumult of the common world; if when you lie down at night your last waking thoughts were—not of your successes, not of your losses, not of your vexations, not of your fears—but of Him? Would that make a great difference to life? I am sure that it would. And I am also sure that if you believed with your whole heart that He died for your sins, this truth would do much to give Him the same great place in your life that He has had in the lives of innumerable saints.

Yes,—this belief, whenever it takes possession of a man, exerts over him a wonderful power. It is Christ and Christ alone who has died for our sins. Others have taught us to live righteously; He and He alone has died because we have lived unrighteously. Others have taught us to love God: He and He alone has died because we have not loved God. If this truth has taken root in us our thoughts cannot escape from it, and therefore they cannot escape from Christ. When conscience condemns us for sin we think of Him; for it is through Him that our sins are to be forgiven. When we are tempted to sin we think of Him, and sin becomes terrible because it was sin that brought upon Him the shame and the anguish and the horror of great darkness through which He passed on the cross. When we are troubled by the sins of other men—when we are appalled by the sins of the race—we think of Him; and we despair of no man, however desperately he has sinned, for Christ died for the sins of the world.

The very mystery of His dying for our sins has an infinite fascination, draws our thoughts to it constantly, and therefore draws our thoughts to Him. No saint—no angel could die for my sins. I stand alone before God, and am myself responsible for my wrong-doing. There can be no transference of my responsibility—no sharing of it. If my sin darkens and desolates the lives of other men, the sufferings and the loss which they endure—voluntarily or involuntarily—as the result of my wrong-doing does not *lessen* the guilt of my offence, but adds to the proof of its malignant power. The more deeply I reflect on the truth that Christ died for me—died for me because I have sinned—and that through His death my sins may be forgiven, the more certain it becomes that between Christ and me there is a kind of relationship that is absolutely unique. He is Another and yet not Another. He can die for me. He, in some wonderful way, is one with me; I, in some wonderful way, am one with Him. And so I may come to be able to say, 'I have been crucified with Christ: yet I live; and yet no longer I, but Christ liveth in me.'

Henceforth all things are possible to me. I have

sinned grievously—but shall I despair of complete recovery from sin—shall I despair of perfection—shall I give way to the horrible dread that I have lost for ever the love of God and the hope of dwelling in His glory? Ah! no. It was in my sin that Christ loved me—and with what amazing love! My sin does not separate me from Him—in my very sin I am bound to Him. It was because I had sinned that He died for me. Now that I am sure of forgiveness through Him I am also sure that through Him I may achieve an eternal victory over sin, and pass into the light of God's eternal Kingdom. Believing this, how can I help thinking of Christ, and thinking of Him always?

The men who have loved Christ with a love that was an overmastering passion—a love that was adoration—a love that rejoiced in suffering for Him, and was eager to undertake the greatest tasks for Him—have been men who believed this gospel that Christ died for their sins. It was this belief that kindled and sustained their love. I do not speak of men who have simply admired Christ and said fine things about Him—what an awful thing it is for sinful men to regard Christ as a Person to be admired and about whom we may say fine things! I am speaking of the men whose love for Christ has been the very life of their life—who have worked for Him, suffered for Him, and when the call came have died for Him; and who have done it all with immeasurable delight;—these were men who believed that

Christ died for their sins. Their belief held them fast to Him. Finding in Him the remission of sins they also found in Him power for all righteousness.

(3) 'He died for our sins;' this is part of the Gospel by which we are saved: 'He hath been raised on the third day'—this is also a part of that Gospel. If we did not know that He has risen again, and that He appeared to the disciples, we should have felt that we had lost Him. We might have supposed that as He had come from God He had been re-absorbed in the Infinite and Eternal Life of God and that He was Son of man no longer. The human Christ would have been a great and august and pathetic memory—nothing more. But we believe that Christ has risen—that He is glorified but still human—that He is Lord of all, yet One who has been in all points tempted like as we are, and yet without sin. We do not envy Peter, James, and John, or Mary and Martha, or any other of His earthly friends. He is nearer to us than He was to them; and He is near to us, not in the limits of His earthly humiliation, but in the power and glory of His eternal life. In our weariness and despondency, when we are tempted, when we have fallen—He is with us still, ready to console, ready to strengthen, ready to forgive. He is with us in all ministries of pity and affection to the poor and the suffering; He is with us in all our endeavours to reclaim the lost. Tell me whether His death for our sins, which binds our hearts to Him, and His resurrection, which assures

us that He is not a dead but a living Christ—tell me whether these are not '*saving truths*'?

Further, Christ's resurrection is the prophecy and assurance of our own ascent to diviner forms of life; if we believe it, we are sure of immortal righteousness and immortal joy. Let me ask whether, if you had perfect faith in the certainty and greatness of the endless life in God, this would not save you from many moral failures by which you are humiliated and distressed?

Our failures have taken many forms. Some of us, perhaps, have been made irritable and impatient by the anxieties and cares of life. One trouble disappears only to give place to another. A man is out of work for six or nine months and gets into debt; and a few weeks after he has begun to work again, and when he is getting a little easy and is paying off one set of small bills after another, he falls ill; or a child has an accident; or a brother dies, and he tries—God bless him!—to do what he can for the widow and children; or there is a strike, and all the trouble comes over again. The man becomes bitter—I do not wonder at it—and resentful, and then his whole life begins to go wrong.

Or you are in business, and disasters descend on you as if you were under some malignant fate. Other men prosper who seem no cleverer than you, and who work no harder; but you are always in difficulties. You lay in a heavy stock just before an unexpected fall of prices. You take a large order from a house which seems as safe as the Bank of England, and just before the bills become due the house stops payment. Your cashier robs you; your best salesman drinks; your manager is bought off by a rival firm; your worries are incessant; and your health is broken by your anxieties.

Or you have come here this morning under the shadow of troubles of another kind. Your husband or your wife is going wrong—seriously wrong; you keep the secret, but you endure misery. Or you have a boy in business in some distant city, and you learnt last week that he has robbed his employer. Or you have a sister or a brother who has come to hate you, and who is slandering you in every direction.

Or, perhaps, your sorrows, though not less keen, are less bitter. The child of your heart is struck for death; or you have discovered that your wife or your husband is suffering from mortal disease. There is no hope, and in a few months all will be over.

And these troubles—or others—for our troubles are infinitely varied—have lowered your moral energy and clouded your moral vision. Suffering does not always make men better than it found them; it sometimes makes them worse. Men in business become desperate and reckless, and determine to save themselves from immediate ruin at any cost; to escape from misfortune they are guilty of crime. In troubles of another description they endeavour to drown their sorrow in drink. Perhaps during the last week some of you were tempted to sin—driven to sin, as you would say—by cruel misfortunes which it seemed impossible for you to bear.

But suppose that beyond the dark and dreary clouds of earthly trouble you had seen the shining splendours of an endless life in God—suppose that this life had been perfectly real to you—suppose that day after day you had held fast to the certainty that the end of all your sorrows would come at last and that then there would be eternal peace—would not the vision and the faith have given you patience, courage, strength, and joy—would they not have saved you from the mental and moral despondency which made you accessible to temptation, just as physical depression makes you accessible to disease?

We are told by some men who are embittered against the Christian Church, that no religion is worth having that does not satisfy the wants and lessen the miseries of mankind in this present world, and that bills drawn on a future heaven are worthless to people who are bankrupt of earthly happiness; and I have seen during the last thirty years an increasing disposition among Christian people themselves to think less and less of the eternal righteousness and eternal joys of the great life to come. I do not wonder that as the result of this, there is less of power and animation in the religious life—less of passion—less of courage—less of the buoyancy which comes from exulting hope. Nor do I wonder that where the Church has almost ceased to preach the

Gospel of an infinite and immortal hope, its power to charm and to attract the hearts of men has been lost. The time was when by patient continuance in well-doing, those who had received the faith of Christ sought for glory, honour, and immortality; when under the strain of severe suffering, and with fainting strength the courage and vigour of the soul were renewed day by day, because poverty and sickness and the heaviest and most protracted of earthly sorrows seemed light and but for a moment when contrasted with the 'eternal weight of glory.'

In days like these when with some the pleasures and luxuries which are at the command of unexampled wealth—though they fail to satisfy the heart, distract it and render it indisposed to seek its perfect rest and joy in God; and when with others the poverty and wretchedness which exist side by side with the magnificence of a splendid civilisation create a bitterness and fierceness of spirit and an angry impatience which destroy faith in the Eternal Justice and the Eternal Love—in days like these there is a supreme call on the Christian Church to recover its ancient faith in the life to come and to proclaim that faith to mankind with its ancient exulting joy.

As a minister of Christ, it is my duty not merely to assure the penitent of God's mercy through Christ, and those who are longing for righteousness of the strength of God to enable them to achieve it—not merely to insist that a religious faith is worthless which does not show its power in kindly services to mankind—not merely to illustrate how the precepts and spirit of Christ are to receive their expression in business, in literature, in art, in the life of the family and the life of the state—not merely to urge on Christian men to secure whatever changes in the social order would bring about a diminution of the misery and an increase of the health, the comfort, the intelligence, the security and the self-respect of those classes of the community whose wretchedness our civilisation has not yet been able to relieve,—but it is also my duty to add a new and infinite sanction to every human duty, and a new and infinite wealth to every divine promise, to open new fountains of consolation to the miserable and new sources of hope to the despairing, to give buoyancy to faith, and vigour to every loyal endeavour to serve God and mankind, by proclaiming that eternal blessedness and glory to which God has destined us in Christ. To every one of you—the poorest and the richest, the happiest and the most wretched—to every one of you those endless ages of power, perfection, and joy transcend in interest all the successes and all the disasters of these mortal years. In God's name I ask whether you intend to lose them—for they may be lost. And to lose them will be appalling ruin, though for threescore years and ten you have enjoyed health and ease, riches, happiness, and honour; to win them will be an infinite compensation for threescore years of poverty and sorrow. Let them fill your imagination —those radiant golden ages—let them kindle your hope, and you will be saved from the worst perils both of earthly wealth and earthly misery.

But how is that great life to become real to us? Paul tells us. He preached that 'Christ died . . . that He was buried'—all hope was lost when they buried Him: the burial was the expression of the despair of those who trusted that He would deliver Israel. But on the third day they found the rocky sepulchre empty—wonderful discovery! And then they learnt that He had been raised from the dead. It was not merely from the angels in the tomb that they learnt it. 'He appeared to Cephas: then to the twelve; then He appeared to above five hundred brethren at once; . . . then . . . to James; then to all the apostles; and last of all,' adds Paul, 'He appeared to me also.' Those who had known and loved Him best saw Him again, and talked with Him. He said wonderful things to them concerning the Kingdom and concerning the great work to which they were destined in making it known to mankind. He came to them when they were together in the upper room at Jerusalem, and when they were together on the shore of the Lake of Galilee. He came to some of them when they were alone. He was the same Jesus to whose discourses they had listened, and whose miracles they had witnessed—the same, yet mysteriously different. He had not returned, like Lazarus, to the life which He had lived before He died. He had escaped from the limitations of our mortal condition. He had ascended to a higher, freer, larger, diviner form of life, and the apostles learnt that this higher life was not only His but ours. And so, to the men who saw Christ after He had risen, the life beyond death was no longer a subject of speculation or of hope or of promise, but of certainty. They had seen it; and what they saw was a large part of their Gospel. Those who received their Gospel shared their certainty; and in these last days, if we receive it, the same certainty will be ours and we shall live under the power of things unseen and eternal. If that would make an immense difference to life—would transfigure and glorify it—is not the resurrection of Christ a '*saving truth*'?

II

This then is the method of the Christian Gospel. This illustrates what Paul meant when he said that the preaching of Christ who was crucified and who rose from the dead—'the foolishness of preaching' as men called it—is the power of God unto salvation. For eighteen centuries the greatness of that power was verified in the history of the Church. The ethical and philosophical teacher may discourse on the evil of sin, may appeal to the conscience to condemn it as a violation of the august and eternal law of righteousness, may warn men of the physical miseries which avenge some forms of vice, may give vivid representations of the wretchedness in families and the confusion and disorder in the state, which are the inevitable results of ambition, indolence, covetousness, injustice, falsehood, treachery. It is all true—and it may be very impressive. But the Christian preacher, while he has said all this, has also said that Christ, the Eternal Son of God, has died for the sins of men. This has been a more effective force in constraining men to abhor sin and to forsake it. It has been the power of God for their salvation.

The ethical and philosophical preacher, seeing as we see, that if men remembered God always and everywhere it would be a great check on sin and a great support to righteousness, may deliver eloquent discourses on God's greatness and goodness, on His nearness to us in all places and at all times, on His direct access to our inner life, His presence *there* as well as in the external world. It is all true and it may be very impressive. But in the Church, for eighteen hundred years, the Christian preacher has also said that the Eternal Son of God has died for men and risen again. When this has been really believed, it has made it impossible for men to forget God. It has been the power of God for their salvation.

It may be clear to the ethical and philosophical teacher that belief in a life beyond death would cool the baser passions of men, would subdue their thirst for wealth, would give them loftier ideals of righteousness, would be a consolation in sorrow and a strong defence against many fierce temptations; and while acknowledging the mysteries of that life he may illustrate the probabilities which point to it. In the Church for eighteen hundred years the Christian preacher has passed from probabilities to certainty. The Christian Gospel declares that Christ rose from the dead and was actually seen by men, again and again, after He had risen. With those who have received this Gospel the powers of the invisible and eternal world have mastered and subdued the powers of this visible and temporal order. They have rejoiced in the hope of the glory of God. The truth that Christ rose from the dead has been the power of God for their salvation.

It is by the living God that we are to be saved, and to suppose that truths—no matter how impressive, how pathetic, how animating, how awful, how glorious—can save us apart from His grace, is one of the worst forms of atheism. But we have learnt from Christ Himself, and from His apostles, that the Gospel is the power of God for their salvation, and if we, to whom that Gospel has been made known, fail to preach it, we are guilty of unfaithfulness both to God and to man. No earnestness of ours in pleading with them to break with sin and to live righteously, to trust in the divine love, and to do the divine will, will avail apart from this. No vague declamation on the love of God will avail. No prayers on their behalf will avail. We may have the most passionate desire to see the whole world covered with a harvest of righteousness and peace; we may entreat God to grant us the harvest; but the 'seed' from which the harvest is to come is 'the Word of God,' and unless we sow it the ground will remain barren.

And so, after all, there is '*saving truth*,'—truth which is a real power in saving men. If any of us are conscious that our salvation is very imperfect, let us ask whether we have a clear and firm understanding of the truths which God means to have a part in effecting our salvation; whether they are laid up in our heart; whether we dwell upon them with love and wonder, and with an eager desire that they may reveal in us the moral and spiritual energy which they have revealed in the perfection of innumerable saints.

Note.—Dr. Martineau has the following observations on the two elements which are present in religion:

'In the soul of Religion, the apprehension of truth and the enthusiasm of devotion inseparably blend: and in proportion as either is deserted by the other, the conditions of right judgment fail. . . . Religion in the old sense above explained' [the sense in which Dr. Martineau uses the word] 'was at once a mode of thought and a mode of feeling; nor does it matter to their indissoluble union which of the two you put into the prior place; whether you trust first the instinct of intuitive reverence, and see the reality of God emerge as its postulate; or whether, having intellectually judged that He is there, you surrender yourself to the awe and love of that infinite presence. . . . It is only an artificial analysis that separates the two and insists on calling the intellectual side of the fact a theology, the affectional a religion. Hence we lose sight of the fact that they are not two things any more than the convex and the concave surface of a curve, but only two aspects of the same thing; and are tempted to think of each as possibly existing without the other, and so to look around us for a religion that may sit apart from all theology.'—*A Study of Religion* (Oxford 1889), vol. i. pages 1-3.

XVI

WHO ARE THE SONS OF GOD?

'*Ye are all sons of God, through faith, in Christ Jesus.*'—GAL. iii. 26.

THE Galatian churches were mainly composed of Gentiles—heathen men and women, who had given up idolatry, and had become believers in one God and in the Lord Jesus Christ, Son of God and Saviour of men. Certain Jewish teachers were insisting that though perhaps their faith in Jesus Christ might be sufficient to save them, they must submit to circumcision and keep the laws of Moses if they wanted to make sure of all the blessedness and glory of the Divine kingdom. The contention was not unlike that of the Roman Catholic Church in later centuries. It is conceded that through the infinite grace of God we Protestant Christians may be saved; but it is suggested that there is something precarious, irregular, abnormal, and incomplete about our salvation, and that if we wish to know the perfect security and perfect blessedness of the Christian redemption we must become incorporate with the Catholic Church, and receive the sacraments from its authorised ministers. Paul's statement of the Judaising teaching is its destruction, 'Are ye so foolish? having begun in the Spirit, are ye now perfected in the flesh?"[1] That, surely, is an inversion of the Divine order. And in the text he inflicts on this pernicious teaching an equally effective blow. In Christ, he says, and through faith, you Gentiles are, *all* of you, sons of God; circumcision can make you nothing greater. You are the sons of God; observing the Jewish law can obtain for you no diviner glory. You are *sons of God* already; what more can you become? In the verses which follow the text he expands this thought, and varies the expression of it. He says, You are incorporate with Christ, the Eternal Son of God; you are members of His body. All the old distinctions that divided man from man and race from race have disappeared; there can be neither Jew nor Greek any longer, neither bond nor free; no male, no female; you are all one man in Christ Jesus. If you are Christ's, then you are Abraham's seed, heirs according to promise—you are *that* already. What can circumcision do for you? Or, to go back to the text, '*Ye are all sons of God—through faith—in Christ Jesus.*'

I.

That is a large and generous Gospel. But does it sound quite right? Does it not strike you as rather poor in contrast with much of the teaching that has been popular in England during the last thirty or forty years? Let us look at the words a little more closely.

[1] Gal. iii. 3.

'*Ye are all sons of God.*' Excellent! So far Paul is clearly right.

'*Through faith*':—but what does that mean? Is not this a narrowing of the Christian Gospel? Are not men *born* sons of God—all men? Do they not *remain* sons of God, always—in this world and the next? Can they ever be anything else, whether they are sinners or saints, believers or unbelievers? It is clear that Paul did not think so. He says plainly enough that men are sons of God '*through faith*'; and if this is true, men who have no faith are not, in Paul's sense, '*sons of God.*'

Let us look at his words again. 'Ye are all sons of God, through faith, *in Christ Jesus.*' Why 'in Christ Jesus'? Are not all men sons of God by nature, whether they are in Christ Jesus or not? Paul says, No: it is only in Christ Jesus that we are sons of God.

But are we not all 'in Christ'? Were we not 'created' in Christ? Is not the whole universe 'held together' in Christ? Yes,—Paul would answer,—for this truth lies at the very foundation of his conception of the relationship between God and the human race—between God and the universe. But in the sense in which he uses the words 'in Christ' in this place, and sometimes elsewhere, all men are not 'in Christ'; and it is only those who are, that are 'sons of God,' in the sense in which Paul is using this glorious title.

We had better look at the contrast between Paul'

teaching and some modern teaching, straight in the face. It is not Paul alone that limits sonship to those who are 'in Christ,' and who have faith in Him. A large part of John's First Epistle is given to an account of the difference—broad, deep, appalling—between men who are God's children and men who are not. Christ Himself, in words more stern and startling than the apostles ever used, peremptorily rejected the claim of some of the Jews to be children of God—rejected it without qualification and without reserve. They said to Him, 'We have one Father, even God.' 'No,' He answered; 'if God were your Father, ye would love Me; for I came forth and am come from God. . . . Ye are of your father the devil, and the lusts of your father ye will do.'

A thorough examination of the writings of the New Testament will show that our Lord Jesus Christ and His apostles represent sonship as a transcendent glory and blessedness which men have to *attain*—not as the common possession and inheritance of all descriptions of men; they identify it with a certain life and character; only those men who possess this life and realise this character are 'sons of God' in the great sense in which they use the words.

Ah!—but you say—'How much finer, how much larger, how much more generous is the teaching which proclaims to all men that they are sons of God.' Proclaim *that*, if you please; but take care that you tell men that this is not what Paul taught—not what John taught—not what Christ taught. Tell them that it distinctly contradicts what Christ and His apostles taught. If what you proclaim is true, do not give Christ credit for it. If it is false, do not charge Him with responsibility for it.

The teaching that all men are the sons of God may seem to you finer, larger, more generous than the teaching that some men are sons and some are not. It may also seem to some persons to be a finer, larger, more generous account of human nature to say that there is no real and grave difference between saint and sinner; that there are imperfections in the greatest of saints and admirable excellencies in the worst of sinners; but though it may be a poor, narrow and ignoble thing to say, still it is true that some men are drunkards, and that some men live soberly; that some are habitual liars, and that some habitually speak the truth; that some are selfish, and some generous; that some are morally coarse, and that some are morally refined; that some are sensual, and some pure. This may seem less beautiful teaching, less generous teaching, less charitable teaching; but it is truer to the facts; and in these great matters it is of the first importance that we should say—not what is pleasant and generous—but what is true.

'Still,' you may reply, 'is it not true that Christ has revealed God as the Father of men?' No doubt: this is one of the glorious distinctions of the Christian Gospel. 'Well, then,' you ask, 'if God is the Father of men, must it not be true that every man is His child?' That is your inference; and the inference is a precarious one; whether it is a sound inference or no, you have to discover from Christ's own teaching; and it appears that when certain men claimed God as *their* Father, He peremptorily denied the claim, and said that their true father was the devil.

It is a glorious truth that God is the Father of men, and in a very real sense the Father of all men. But all human relationships are inadequate illustrations of the relationship between God and man—between man and God. God is our Father, but we must be careful how we argue from the human relationship to the divine. For example, suppose I were to reason in this way: A son shares his father's life, and may in the course of a very few years become his father's equal, and even his father's superior, in physical strength, in keenness of intellect, in soundness of judgment, in moral goodness. This is of the very essence of the relationship between son and father. If I am a son of God, I, too, may in the course of a few years—or, at least, in the course of ages—become God's equal or even God's superior. If not, He is not my Father and I am not His son. Would that conclusion be sound? It follows directly from the relationship of a human son to a human father. If there were never in a son the capacity for growth up to the height of the father's power and goodness;—if the growth were always and necessarily arrested so as to keep an immense distance between father and son, the nature of the relationship would be wholly changed.

All human analogies intended to illustrate the relation between God and ourselves or between ourselves and God, must be imperfect. They are true at one point, perhaps at two points, perhaps at three; but as soon as we begin to establish truths on analogy alone we are in danger of grave mistakes.

II.

What, then, is the truth on this great subject?

1. It is true that we are 'God's offspring.' We derive our life from Him; we have moral freedom; we have understanding, reason, conscience. All these are indications of the greatness of our origin and of our *natural* kinship to the Supreme. But this relationship, according to the teaching of the Lord Jesus Christ and His apostles—though very wonderful—is but the condition of a relationship far more wonderful and glorious. And it is to those who realise this higher relationship that they habitually restrict the great title 'Sons of God.'

2. For the highest glory of God is His moral perfection—His righteousness, His purity, His compassion, His truth, His infinite love; and His moral perfection is the eternal flower of His eternal life.

There is nothing new in *that*: you have heard it very often before; but will you *think* about it for a few minutes? The highest glory of God is His moral perfection; and His moral perfection is, I say, the eternal flower of His eternal life. You and I may be righteous or unrighteous, and still remain men; but *it belongs to the very life of God to be righteous.* You and I may be pure or impure, and still remain men; but *it belongs to the very life of God to be pure.* You and I may be holy or unholy, and still remain men; but *it belongs to the very life of God to be holy.* You and I may be cruel or compassionate, and still remain men; but *it belongs to the very life of God to be compassionate.* You and I may be selfish or unselfish, and still remain men; but *it belongs to the very life of God to love.*

Yes; you know all that. But will you *think* of it a little longer? It is the things we know that we have most need to think about.

It belongs, I say, to the very life of God to be just, merciful, pure, compassionate, loving, holy; if then He ceased to be just, merciful, pure, compassionate, loving, holy, He would descend from the heights of Godhead—awful thought! to abysses of darkness and eternal night. Righteousness and judgment—as an ancient saint discovered—are the foundations of His throne; let the righteousness become injustice and the judgment lawlessness, and His throne would break up and perish. He would be God no longer. Almighty power, infinite knowledge, eternal existence, omnipotence—these would not avail to maintain His divine Majesty. He would cease to be God, for the life of God would be His no longer.

3. Now for another step. If we share the life of God—His highest life,—we, too, shall be just, pure, compassionate, holy, loving. As He would cease to have His highest life if He ceased to be good—we do

not share His highest life unless we are good. His life cannot be ours unless we live it; and the life in *us*—as in God—is an active force revealing itself in righteousness, goodness, holiness. It may be very feeble in us for a time; but if it is in us at all, it is working for our moral and spiritual perfection; and from its origin and characteristic quality it will be the highest force in us—not one of the inferior powers struggling against extinction among the confused impulses and instincts of the lower provinces of our nature.

4. And now we are prepared to grasp the teaching of the New Testament concerning what it is to be sons of God. To be sons of God we must share the life of God, and the life of God is a life of righteousness, purity, compassion, holiness, love. Where these are not, the life of God is not. Where these are not, men are not in the great sense the sons of God; for those who have not the life of God cannot be His sons.

III.

There is hardly a truth more deeply wrought into the substance of the New Testament than this. It appears in many forms; it is enforced by many illustrations; it is involved in doctrine and precept, in promise and warning. To reject it is to break up the coherence of the whole teaching of our Lord Jesus Christ and His apostles.

There is one striking proof of the deep impression

which it made on the ancient Church. In the fourth and fifth centuries—probably earlier—only believers in Christ who had been received into the full communion of the Church were taught the Lord's Prayer and allowed to be present at services where it was offered. For heathen men to call God 'Our Father' was, in the judgment of the Church of those days, a profanation. Even the catechumens, who were persons receiving religious instruction as a preparation for baptism, were not allowed to offer it. Not until a man was believed to be regenerate of the Holy Ghost was he permitted to regard himself as a son of God and to call God Father.

That, too, while it illustrates the vividness with which the Church had apprehended the truth, that it is only to those who receive Christ—'even to them that believe on His name'—that Christ gives 'the right to become children of God,' is also an illustration of the error which may come from drawing inferences from analogies. The ancient Church began by saying, Only those who have received the life of God by regeneration are, in the great sense which Christ has given to the words, 'sons of God.' That is true. But the inference was drawn that only those who have received the life of God by regeneration have the right to call God Father. That is false. The modern error is the precise converse of this. It begins by saying, God is the Father of all men. That is true. It infers that all men are God's sons. That is false.

We were created to be God's sons—God's sons in the great and glorious sense in which we are His sons when we receive that life of God which is a life of righteousness, purity, compassion, holiness, and love. But the relation, though having its basis in a mere natural relationship, is ethically and spiritually realised. It belongs to the spiritual order in which the physical omnipotence of God has no place. It is realised in the free, unforced choice of perfection on our part; without that choice it is impossible and inconceivable. We *become* sons when we receive the life of God and live in the power of it. If that life is received it must be lived; in failing and refusing to live it we fail and refuse to be sons.

IV

But the failure is on our side, not on God's side. All that He can do to realise His own will and purpose concerning the relationship between us He has done. He has created us with the capacity for receiving His own eternal life. He has so created us that we do not reach the perfection and harmony of our nature till we receive it. He disquiets and troubles us, allows us no enduring peace, until we receive it. He presses the supreme gift upon us in a thousand ways, entreats and commands us to receive it. He appeals to our conscience and to our fears to induce us to receive it. He kindles in our imagination fair ideals of goodness which it is impossible for us to achieve until we receive it. He reveals His own perfect righteousness which illustrates the glory of the life, in order to prevail upon us to receive it. He tells us of the blessedness, perfection, and power—the blessedness, perfection, and power of the sons of God—for which He has created us and to which He has destined us, but which we can never attain unless we receive it. That we might have redemption from our sins, Christ, the Eternal Son, has descended from divine heights and died for us all. He is eager to forgive. As far as the east is from the west, so far is He ready to remove our transgressions from us. He, for His part, will be our Father—nothing less. On His side the relationship exists as far as it can exist without our concurrence and consent; and, therefore, we may call Him Father, even though as yet we are not sons. For this, I repeat, is the relation in which He is resolved to stand to us. He will stand in no other. If we persistently and finally refuse to be sons, then all relationship between Him and us must be dissolved, and there must be eternal separation.

V

The question to which I have been endeavouring to give an answer—Who are the sons of God?—is not a question for theologians only—a question lying remote from life and having no interest except for a speculative curiosity. It concerns the present moral character of men; it concerns their eternal salvation. And if we yield to some of the strongest currents of contemporary thought we shall give an answer to it which contradicts the plainest teaching of our Lord and of His apostles.

John says, 'In this the children of God are manifest, and the children of the devil: whosoever doeth not righteousness is not of God, neither he that loveth not his brother.'[1] No—we are told—the unrighteous man is just as truly a child of God as the righteous; and the man that hates his brother is just as truly a child of God as the man whose heart is full of love.

'Whosoever believeth that Jesus is the Christ,' says John, 'is born of God.' Yes, it is answered, and whosoever believeth not that Jesus is the Christ is also born of God. The belief makes no difference. What John says is therefore misleading.

'As many as received Him,' says John, 'to them gave He the right to become children of God, even to them that believe on His name.'[2] Impossible! it is replied; for they were children of God before they received Him and before they believed on Him—disobedient children, perhaps; unhappy children—children who did not know the greatness of their birth, and who had sunk into misery through not knowing it; but still children. All men are God's children by their very birth. How could Christ give to those who believed Him 'the *right* to *become* children of God'? It was theirs before they believed.

'Whatsoever is begotten of God overcometh the

[1] 1 John iii. 10. [2] John i. 12.

world,'[1] says John again. No, it is answered, even though a man is wholly mastered by its pleasures, its honours, its wealth, or its calamities, he is as truly a son of God as the most victorious saint.

The two forms of teaching are directly contradictory. If one is true, the other must be false.

It is by being 'born again' that men become in the great sense children of God. 'That which is born of the flesh is flesh, and that which is born of the Spirit is spirit,'[2] and 'Except a man be born anew, he cannot see the kingdom of God.'[3] That is Christ's teaching; it is met by the declaration that every man by his natural birth is a son of God, and therefore the heir of eternal glory. I say again—the two forms of teaching are directly contradictory; if one is true, the other must be false.

I should not wonder if it is in part the result of this teaching that large numbers of men who are regularly present in Christian congregations miss the infinite blessings which God has conferred on the race in Christ. They have never been told—they have never discovered the immense difference between that merely natural relationship to God on the ground of which all men may be described as His 'offspring' and that ethical and spiritual sonship which implies the actual realisation of the life of God in character and conduct. The assumption that all men are God's children—God's children in the same

[1] 1 John v. 4. [2] John iii. 6. [3] John iii. 3.

sense, whether believers or unbelievers, saints or sinners—underlies all their religious thought. Since, as they assume, they are God's children in the very same sense in which John and Paul and Peter were His children, it is impossible for them to have any other final home than the eternal glory of their Father. The assumption breaks the force of every terrible warning that came from the lips of Christ and the apostles; if they are the children of God, it is impossible that they should eternally perish. Ah, yes; but suppose that they are *not* the children of God—what then?

The assumption is a moral anodyne; it subdues and dulls the moral pain that comes from the consciousness of sin; for surely, sooner or later, God's children will become perfectly like Him; whatever imperfection may now trouble them need not give them serious alarm. God will make His children perfectly righteous in the next world, if not in this. Ah, yes! but suppose that they are *not* God's children?

I entreat you to look at Christ's teaching and the teaching of His Apostles; no Gospel, which professes to be more gracious and more generous than theirs can be a true Gospel. I entreat you not to imagine that the infinite contrast between good and evil has ceased to exist, or has become less appalling than when Christ and His Apostles spoke to men about judgment to come, and the contrasted destinies of the saved and the lost. I entreat you not to suppose that God, apart from your own choice, apart from your own strenuous effort, apart from prayer and self-discipline and constant vigilance, can bring you to everlasting perfection and glory. God is infinitely merciful! Yes, and His infinite mercy has redeemed you in Christ. I entreat you not to take it for granted that you can remain indifferent to that supreme effort of His mercy and yet be redeemed. That is the final achievement of God's infinite grace; we can imagine nothing beyond it. In Christ God has made His great appeal to the heart, the conscience, and the reason of man; resist that, and you pass beyond the reach of those moral and spiritual forces by which alone you can be saved. Christ is the propitiation for the sin of the world; there is no other; reject Him, and 'there remaineth no more any sacrifice for sin, but a certain fearful expectation of judgment, and a fierceness of fire which shall devour the adversaries.'

The choice before us is an awful one. We were created to be sons of God, but if we reject our destiny it cannot be forced upon us. If we do not elect to be children of the Eternal, God's election of us is defeated. And if we miss the greatness for which we were created, persistent consciousness will be persistent misery. We are wholly unfitted for a life of inferior dignity. There can be nothing for us but the anguish and horror of discovering our infinite loss—and then the silence and darkness of eternal death.

But I will not believe that you can be content to lose it. Think of the glory of having the life of God—the life in the power of which He is eternal Righteousness, eternal Purity, eternal Holiness, eternal Love. Think of the blessedness of being, in deed and of a truth, sons of God, conscious of kinship to Him, living in His presence, defended from harm by His eternal protection, happy for ever in His infinite grace. This is the blessedness for which you were created; and though you have sinned it is not irrecoverably lost; in Christ it is yours still; resolve to make it actually your own.

I fear that one great reason why the moral life of many slumbers, so that they make no effort to rise to the dignity of sons of God, is their belief that the dignity is theirs apart from their own choice, and that it cannot be lost by their own negligence and sin.

Fatal error! There is nothing really great or good that becomes effectively ours apart from our own effort. You may be born with the genius of an artist or poet; but you will not be an artist or poet unless your genius, which is a quality and power of life, energetically exerts itself and so realises its glory. You may be born with a great faculty for scientific discovery; but unless there is patience and persistent effort in the actual exertion of the faculty you will never be a scientific discoverer. To mere external things—to external wealth and rank, for example—you may be born; you may enjoy them without effort; but the wealth and the rank which are not external but personal,—these must be personally achieved.

This is supremely true in morals and religion. You cannot be truthful, just, pure by birth merely; you must achieve these virtues by a virtuous life. Nor can you be sons of God by birth merely. For the sonship is ethical and spiritual—not merely natural. You were created that it might be yours; but you have to realise it '*in Christ*' and '*by faith*,' in the power of the Spirit of God and the grace of Christ Jesus our Lord. I entreat you by the infinite love of God, who longs to have you for His sons—I entreat you by the transcendent perfection, blessedness and glory which will be yours if you actually become His sons, and by the infinite loss and shame you must incur if you do not—to resolve, in the strength of God, that this sonship shall be yours.

XVII

PERSONAL RESPONSIBILITY

'*So then each one of us shall give account of himself to God.*'
ROMANS xiv. 12.

THERE is a sentence in one of Mr. Emerson's essays which, when I was a young man, sent a thrill through me like an electric shock: 'Trust thyself. Every heart vibrates to that iron string.' Many years have passed since I first read those words, but even now the vividness of the impression which they produced has hardly diminished. I am not quite sure that in these days the human heart vibrates to that iron string just as it did thirty or forty years ago, when to young and ardent men Mr. Emerson's essays seemed almost a new gospel. The curious blending of stoicism and mysticism in Mr. Emerson's thought has lost its spell, and has given place to a Sensational and Epicurean philosophy which is unfriendly to that appeal to the intuitions and forces of the individual soul which recurs so constantly in his essays. This change in the currents of speculation affects us all, and is exerting a growing influence both on morals and on religious belief. To defend and to reinforce those elements of moral and religious strength which are becoming enfeebled, something beyond Mr. Emerson's stoicism and mysticism is necessary. We must reassert that great truth which in all the ages of Christendom has had so much to do with the loftier and more robust forms of personal righteousness. There was never a time when it was safe for the Church to forget the Judgment to come. But this august and solemn revelation receives an altogether exceptional importance from the speculative and moral tendencies of our own time. The revelation of Judgment to come is one of the chief guarantees of human morality, and one of the most impressive illustrations of human greatness.

Are we not in danger,—all of us,—of losing the vivid sense of personal responsibility for our own life? And if the sense of personal responsibility is lost, reverence for the stern and beneficent authority of duty is lost too. There can be no morality apart from moral freedom, and the idea of moral freedom has sensibly become less and less distinct during the last thirty or forty years. It is not merely faith in the Christian revelation and in the living God which is menaced by the popular philosophy. The spirit of Scientific Imperialism,—the illegitimate endeavour to carry the authority of physical forces and unvarying law beyond the limits of the material universe, and to enthrone them over every province of human life and activity,—is destructive of the difference between right and wrong. Deny the moral freedom of individual men, and henceforth there is nothing in human conduct to condemn, nothing to approve, nothing to brand with ignominy, nothing to celebrate with praise. The difference vanishes between the honest man and the scoundrel, the truthful man and the liar, the brutal and the kindly, the coward and the hero, the patriot and the tyrant. All are alike the products—the necessary products—of the vast and unconscious forces of the universe. The tragedy and the glory, the shame and the honour, of human life are gone.

I have no fear that this conception of human life will win a lasting ascendency. The literature and the history of all past centuries condemn it. It is condemned by all that is most generous in human nature. It offers no explanation of the most splendid and most awful experiences of human life. It gives no account of the eternal fame which has been won by heroic goodness, of the eternal execration which follows exceptional crime. It gives no account of the passionate thrill of affection and honour with which a whole nation witnesses some act of courageous self-sacrifice, no account of the deep and indignant abhorrence with which it listens to the story of some act of base and cruel villainy. It does not explain the peace of heart which follows personal righteousness, the agony of remorse which often follows outrageous wrong-doing. All these are just as real as the motions of the planets or the rise and fall of the tides. They are inexplicable except on the hypothesis that man is free to choose between the noble and the base, between the right and the wrong; and the nobleness and the righteousness of the true choice are heightened by the strength of the motives which might have induced him to choose differently.

Now, it is to this individual freedom that the revelation of future judgment appeals. Your life,—the moral character of your life,—is in your own hands, and for that the righteous and eternal God will hold you, one by one, accountable. Nearly everything else has been determined for you, and is beyond the control of your will; but for your moral conduct you yourselves are responsible. Most of us, I suppose, had very little freedom of choice as to the trade or the profession that we should follow; but we can work honestly or dishonestly in the actual trade or profession in which we are engaged. We could not choose our work; but we can choose whether we will be industrious or idle in the doing of it. We could not determine what our secular engagements should be; but we can make this great election—whether in these secular engagements we will recognise first of all, always and everywhere, the will of God as supreme.

I suppose it does not altogether depend upon a man whether he will be a skilful workman or a clumsy workman. Some men are born with a flexibility and a strength of muscle, a keenness of eye, a delicacy of taste—or rather, with the possibility of achieving these things—of which other men are naturally destitute, and to which they can never attain. But every man can do his best, whatever that best may be.

It does not lie in our choice what language we shall speak, but it does lie in our choice whether we will speak the truth or whether we will be indifferent to the claims of truthfulness; whether our language shall be profane or devout, whether it shall be pure or impure.

We had no choice into what kind of family we should be born—whether our parents, our brothers, our sisters, should be rough or gentle, just or unjust; but as we had no choice concerning what kind of family we should be born into, we have to give no account of them. We have to give account of ourselves. It lies with us—whether they are rough or gentle, whether they are just or unjust—to treat them with justice and with kindness.

The limits of our physical health and vigour are determined for us by the circumstances in which we were born, but it lies with ourselves to determine whether we will be sober or drunkards, whether we will be gluttonous or temperate.

It did not lie within our choice whether we would be born in a heathen or a Christian land, among Romanists or among Protestants; but it does lie within every man's choice whether he will honour and welcome whatever light comes to him from the upper heaven—the dim light which is not altogether quenched in Pagan countries, the clearer light which struggles through the dense clouds of Roman error, the open glory which shines from the life and teaching of the Lord Jesus Christ. A man's relation to the invisible and eternal world—to the higher regions of human hope and destiny—to the living God,—a man's relationship to these is not determined by the amount of light that reaches him, but by his reception of it. 'This is the condemnation, that light has come into the world, and men have loved darkness rather than light, because their deeds are evil.'

We know that these are but the commonplaces of Christian morality. But I fear that in some of us—in many of us in these days—the sense of our personal responsibility is faint and feeble. We are surrounded by an immense and wonderful material universe, and its minutest atoms as well as its suns and stars are governed by fixed and unvarying laws. Year after year scientific discovery wins fresh triumphs over regions previously unknown, and everywhere the reign of law is undisturbed. Through ages which we cannot measure, the great forces which are expressed in the phenomena of the material universe have been constant, and the laws which control their action uniform. Even those of us who have no special acquaintance with physical science feel the solemn spell of this immense and immovable order. Sometimes we have no strength to stand erect in its presence. We are awed by the vast range and the irresistible action of material forces. What are we, that we should assert a freedom that does not belong to the planets or to the ocean?

But I decline to surrender my dignity in the presence of material immensity. The tides rise and fall by an eternal necessity, but the passions which ebb and flow in my heart I can check and control. The planets are bound by irreversible forces to the orbits in which they travel, but I am often conscious of perplexity as to the line in which I should move; and instead of being irresistibly swung by a force over which I have no control, I choose for myself the rough path of duty, which leads to mountain heights where I breathe the air of heaven, and see its glory—or the smoother path which descends to darkness and death. I am greater than the planets, I am greater than the sea. They are subject: I am sovereign. They submit: I rule. They are bound: I am free. My own consciousness assures me of this, and it is confirmed by the voice of God. From behind and above the forces of the material universe, there reaches me a word which recognises my unique prerogative, isolates me from all material things, imposes on me the responsibility of my moral action. The living God who is above Nature, tells me that I too am above Nature, and that I must give account of myself to Him.

Then the physiologist comes, and he tells me that I inherit in my very blood, in the very structure of my brain, in the vigorous or feeble fibre of my nervous organisation, the results of the vices and the virtues of a long line of ancestors. No doubt: but what do you mean by vices and by virtues, the results of which I inherit? Are these names of honour and of dishonour, names of praise and condemnation? If there was vice in my ancestors, there may be vice in me. If there was virtue in them, there may be virtue in me. But where there is necessity there is neither virtue nor vice.

This doctrine of heredity is no new discovery. Why, men must have seen from the very dawn of human history that parents transmit to their children, not merely their outward form and features, but many of the moral tendencies of their nature. And this doctrine of heredity was one of the chief articles of the Christian creed for many centuries, and was stated in a form which justly provoked fierce moral resentment. The doctrine of Original Sin was the theological anticipation of the scientific doctrine of heredity, just as the doctrine of Monotheism was the theological anticipation of the scientific doctrine of the unity of the material universe and the universal supremacy of law. The theological doctrine of Original Sin we have now come to see—most of us, at least, have come to see—was a gross exaggeration of the truth. The scientific doctrine of heredity has been made the basis of speculations which are also a gross exaggeration of the truth. Scientists have but trodden in the paths which theologians have been wise enough to forsake, and are repeating the errors which theologians, under the constraint of man's moral nature, have long ago renounced.

It is true that the whole conditions of my life have

been determined for me by my ancestors. My strength of muscle, the soundness of my heart and lungs, the limits of my intellectual capacity, have all been settled for me by my birth. And as the result of the moral character of my ancestors my moral life is one of comparative ease or of severe difficulty. But though the conditions of life have been determined for me, my life itself is my own, and that has not been determined for me. The material with which I should work has been given,—the way in which I should treat it has not been given. I may have been born sluggish: I have to determine whether I will yield or not to my natural tendency to sluggishness. I may have been born with susceptibility to violence of temper: it does not follow that my temper is to be violent; I have to determine whether I will struggle with my susceptibility, and subdue and chain down the temper which would hurry me into many grievous offences. I may have been born with a tendency to sullenness and to gloom: but listening to the teaching of the Christian faith and discovering that joy is an element of Christian perfection, it becomes just as much my duty to struggle against sullenness and gloom as to struggle against any gross sensual vice, and I must set my whole heart and strength to resist and subdue my natural tendency. I may have been born with a craving for physical excitement. Is that to be my excuse if I come home drunk? God forbid. The craving has to be wrestled with, smitten down. I have so to discipline myself that that craving shall be continually checked.

And to God—to God—some of the noblest forms of moral life may be found where to your eyes and to mine there is the least dignity and grace. You were born under felicitous circumstances; but to reach the virtue which you attained without effort, another man may have to exert incessant energy. His dearly bought excellence, though inferior to that which you have easily achieved, is to God infinitely nobler and more precious than the goodness which you, without effort, have accomplished. Each man has to '*give account of himself to God.*'

One man is placed under conditions—conditions not of his own choice, conditions to which he was destined—which make it possible for him to do very little beyond getting the rough ore of goodness out of the black and gloomy mine. He has got it with the sweat of his brow, with pain, with peril. To him God will say, 'Well done!' Another man has the ore at his feet to start with. It is not enough for him to bring that to God. For him there is a different task. In the fires of self-discipline he has to liberate the ore from its dross, and to produce the pure metal. It is enough that one man should bring the rough ore to God; this man must bring pure metal extracted from it. And a third has the metal to begin with. He fails, and fails disastrously, unless he works it up into forms of noble usefulness and gracious beauty. Each man will have to '*give account of himself to God,*' and only God can judge of the worth of each man's work, because only God knows the conditions under which each man's work is being carried on. I suppose that the words which came to the lips of one of the school-fellows of William Ellery Channing sometimes come to the lips of other children on this side of the Atlantic, and the thought which they express has come into the minds of many who are no longer children. When Channing was a very little boy, his schoolmaster said to one of his school-fellows, 'Why are you not a good child like William Channing?' 'Oh,' said the boy, 'it is so easy for William Channing to be good.' We, perhaps, have looked round upon friends of ours to whom the conflict we have to maintain is altogether unnecessary. The foes we have to fight with they never meet. The victories which we have to win for ourselves were won for them generations ago by the ancestors whose blood is in their veins. Shall we complain? God forbid. Let us do for posterity what their ancestors have done for them, taking the rough conditions of our actual life, making the best of them, winning no praise from men for what we accomplish —for they know not the difficulty of the work— rejoicing in this humbly and reverently, that we have to give account of ourselves to God.

Yes, *to God.* We are not under a rigid law. We are under personal authority, acting in harmony with the eternal principles of law; and we have to meet a personal judgment, whose decision will be determined by the eternal principles of law. But this is the supreme thing, that only a living person who knows us altogether can appreciate the true conditions under which our moral life has been lived, the heights we ought to have reached, and the grounds on which we may be forgiven for not having reached heights which were easily accessible to others.

We have to give account, each one of himself, to God; and it is this conception of the relations between man and God, and this alone, which for me relieves human life of its awful gloom and confusion, and contains the promise of a divine order. You tell me that there are great masses of men that have never had a chance of moral goodness. They have to give account of themselves without their chance, if so it be. God knows how large their chance was, and how small. Do not resent by anticipation the justice of the Eternal. He will deal with them according to their conditions. 'Virtue is impossible to them,' you say. Yes, yours. And there are others who, as they look upon you, say, 'Virtue is impossible to you.' Their virtue is. And yet you and I, under the hard conditions of our life, can choose the better path, however feebly we may walk in it; and who but God can tell what glimmerings of light reach those who seem to sit in outer darkness? How rarely it happens that any man can be found, under any conditions, who will not respond at some point to a moral appeal that is made to him by his fellow-man. And if there be this sensitiveness to the appeal that comes from us even in those that look the most degraded, who will deny that where we fail to secure response God may see whether the light that comes to them is welcomed, faint and dim as it may be, or whether it is rejected? We know who He is who is 'the Light of every man.' Where the Light is welcomed, Christ is welcomed; where the Light is rejected, Christ is rejected.

And this conception of our relationship to God invests with dignity, with infinite grandeur, the life alike of the obscurest and most illustrious of our race. It is this, and this alone, which will save Christendom from the moral degradation which would follow the triumph of theories, falsely called scientific, which during the last quarter of a century have been gaining ascendency. Men are becoming cowards in the presence of the material forces of which they are the princes. The spirit of slaves is corrupting them. They creep and crawl in the dust, and with a base, contemptible oblivion of their true dignity, are declaring that they have neither sceptre nor crown; that they are subject, like the material creation of which they claim to be a part, to forces which they cannot control. No regal virtues will be illustrated by a man or a nation that has abdicated regal dignity. There will be no high achievement, no daring, no self-sacrifice; nothing of the force by which time after time in the history of the world that history has been compelled to take a new and loftier direction. Even the material triumphs of which we are so proud, are the result of a spiritual energy which has come to us from generations which believed that man was the lord of all. And when that consciousness of sovereignty has been extinguished, we shall cease to be masters even of the world at our feet; and, losing all our force and fire, all our imperial ways, we shall decline to meaner levels and to inferior forms of life.

But this is not to be our destiny. We are free, and we know it. And if to this freedom there are mysterious limitations,—if achievement hesitates, and falters, and follows far behind purpose, the Christian Gospel has its word of power and of grace for us in this great trouble. Yes, we are free; and yet how conscious at times we are of chains—chains some of which we have forged ourselves by evil-doing in years gone by. We choose the right, and for more than two thousand years moralists have said we are unable to stand to our choice. Yes, free—free, and yet in chains. To be conscious that we are bound is to be conscious that we are free, that in our own inner life there is a spontaneous self-asserting force which claims the right, even though it may not have the power, to work out its own destiny. Christ came to 'preach deliverance to the captive, and the opening of the prison to them that are bound,' and in age after age, in our own time as in times gone by, men have listened to His voice, have believed His promise, hoping it might be true, and in response to hope rather than to faith Christ has come—has come as the angel came to Peter sleeping in his chains between the two soldiers, and at the touch of an invisible hand the chains have fallen away and the man has become free.

We have to give account of ourselves to God. How is it, my brother, between you and Him? You can tell. Deal with yourself honestly, and you can discover how it stands between you and Him. He claims supreme authority over life,—over your life with all its provinces of activity. You may not be able to tell whether you are fulfilling His thought concerning what your life should be, but you can tell this—whether to do that is the real meaning and purpose of your life. You can tell whether from your very heart you have accepted the will of the Eternal as the supreme law of conduct. And every man can see that it is the reasonable, and the right, and the blessed thing so to accept His will. Conscious of failure, of fault, of defeat in conflict after conflict, troubled at coming short of your own ideal of righteousness, you can tell whether you are troubled most by this—that you have come short of God's ideal of righteousness, and whether to you there is infinite joy, infinite hope, in the assurance that it is in His heart to grant you remission of sins. You can tell without difficulty whether you care for the Divine forgiveness. You know the aids to the perfect life which are within reach of us all, and which are among the supreme gifts of Christ to the race. You can tell whether, being conscious of personal weakness, you have not accepted personal weakness as an excuse for failure in righteousness, but have rather said, 'While the strength of God is accessible to me, all righteousness is possible.' When we give account of ourselves to God, must not these three questions be dealt with?—

Have we seriously accepted His will as the law of our life?

Are we eager to receive His pardon for not having perfectly loved and perfectly obeyed Him?

Have we, with intense and persistent earnestness, endeavoured to ally our weakness with His strength, and to receive into our very life the power which has enabled the saints of all generations to achieve righteousness?

No weakness is an excuse for sin, while the weakest can receive the strength of God in order to break with sin and to do His will. May God help us so to live that it shall be possible for us, one by one, to go and give a good account of ourselves to Him.

XVIII

A SERVANT OF JESUS CHRIST

'*A servant of Jesus Christ.*'—ROM. i. 1.

THESE words may assist us to find a practical working answer to a question by which I suppose that many of us have been perplexed in past years, and by which some of us may be perplexed this morning.

First, I will state the question. The teaching of our Lord Jesus Christ and His apostles divides all men into two great classes, and declares that between those who belong to the one class and those who belong to the other there are the widest contrasts both in their present condition and their future destiny. What is it that makes this critical difference between one man and another,—a difference which affects his present relation to God, and which determines whether he is to gain or to lose immortal righteousness and glory?

Morally, the lives of men shade off by the finest gradations from a stainless and heroic virtue to the grossest and meanest vice. The extremes of goodness and of wickedness are very remote from each other and can be easily distinguished; they are as unlike as clear sunshine and a dark, moonless, starless night. But most men are neither extremely good nor extremely wicked. The characters of some are strangely mixed; they have conspicuous virtues and also conspicuous vices. Other men seem to be too feeble to be either virtuous or vicious: the moral habits of some men, again, seem to have been formed, partly by their physical temperament, partly by their early education and the external conditions of their later years; they appear to have no independent life of their own. To draw a sharp and decisive line between those who are morally good and those who are morally bad is impossible. Throwing out of consideration the two extremes, all that we can say of the rest of mankind is—not that some of them are good and others bad—but that some are better and some are worse than others.

But religiously—according to the teaching of Christ and His apostles,—the case is wholly different. Men are either definitely on the side of Christ, or definitely against Him. In the account which our Lord gives of the judgment of the nations, the righteous stand on the right side of the Judge, and the unrighteous on the left; there is no intermediate position. From other parts of His teaching we learn that among the righteous there will be gradations of honour and reward; and that those who have shown the greatest love for God and man will inherit the greatest glory. On the other hand, among the condemned there will be gradations of penalty; and those who have had the largest knowledge of the will of God and have not done it will be punished with the severest doom. And yet there is an immense and awful contrast between all the saved and all the lost; there is no intermediate destiny.

What is it—this is the question I want to answer—what is it that makes this critical difference between one man and another?

Many of you are prepared to answer the question at once:—You quote a text: 'As Moses lifted up the serpent in the wilderness, even so must the Son of Man be lifted up: that whosoever believeth may in Him have eternal life.'[1] These are the words of Christ Himself, and they are final. John, in repeating the words, develops their meaning in the great words which, I suppose, have revealed to countless millions of men the way to perfection and eternal blessedness:—'For God so loved the world that He gave His only begotten Son, that whosoever believeth on Him should not perish, but have eternal life.'[2] Faith in Christ—it is this which makes the infinite difference between the living and the dead, between those whose sins are forgiven and those who are under the divine condemnation, between the lost and the saved.

These are not isolated sentences unsupported by the concurrent teaching of other parts of the New Testament. That faith in the Lord Jesus Christ is

[1] John iii. 14, 15.

[2] John iii. 16.

the critical and decisive act of the soul,—the act as the result of which it passes into the light and life of God,—belongs to the very substance of the teaching both of our Lord Jesus Christ Himself and of His Apostles. It was the re-assertion of this great truth by the Reformers that renewed the religious and moral life of Northern Europe three centuries and a half ago.

This answer to the question which we are considering is not only absolutely true; it seems to many of us perfectly simple. But I remember the time very well, though it is nearly fifty years ago, when this simple truth, that if I believed in Christ it would make an infinite difference to me, was unintelligible. It perplexed and confounded me. Did I not believe in Christ already? I thought I did, and yet I was very sure that nothing had come of it. I used to look at such words as those of Paul to the jailer at Philippi: 'Believe on the Lord Jesus, and thou shalt be saved;'[1] I thought that I believed, but I was certain that I was not saved. The trouble lasted for many months; night after night when the house was still, I read and thought and prayed and endeavoured to discover the secret of my failure and disappointment. I thought that, perhaps, if I believed in Christ at all I did not believe in the right way; but then, how was I to discover the right way? This sent me off on metaphysical adventures which yielded no discoveries of the kind I wanted. Then I thought

[1] Acts xvi. 31.

that, perhaps, I was not believing on the right grounds, and I attempted to repair and strengthen the foundations of my faith; but this, too, was without any good result. At last—how, I cannot tell—it all came clear; I ceased thinking of myself and of my faith, and thought only of Christ; and then I wondered that I should have been perplexed for even a single hour.

It may be inconsiderately suggested that all my trouble came from the theologians who have discriminated between different kinds of faith, and that in the early times, before theology existed, men had no difficulty at all in understanding what was meant by believing in Christ. It is true, no doubt, that when Paul told the people of Thessalonica and Corinth and Ephesus that if they believed in Christ they would receive the forgiveness of sin and the power to live a righteous life, and would become the heirs of eternal glory, they asked for no account of the nature of faith, nor did they attempt to discuss whether their own faith was of the right kind. They believed, and they were saved.

But in their case the reality of their belief was subjected immediately to a severe test. They were required to submit to Christian baptism, and by submitting to baptism they broke with their old life, and cast in their fortunes with a sect which was universally regarded with distrust, with unfriendliness, and at times with fierce hostility.

The heathen man when he was baptized had to

forsake the worship of his fellow-countrymen, to separate himself from a large part of their social life, to cease to observe many prevailing customs, to accept a new law of conduct. The Jew when he was baptized was abhorred by other Jews as a traitor to his race. A secret unavowed faith was never recognised by the apostles as sufficient. 'If thou shalt confess with thy mouth Jesus as Lord, and shalt believe in thy heart that God raised Him from the dead, thou shalt be saved: for with the heart man believeth unto righteousness; and with the mouth confession is made unto salvation.'[1] It might be assumed that the faith which did not shrink from the perils and obligations of confessing Christ in those days was a real faith.

And yet, even then, there was the possibility of self-deception. It was not a theologian that began to distinguish between one kind of faith and another; nor was the distinction made in the interest of theology. It was James,—James who insisted almost exclusively on the obligation of moral duty,—that contrasted a living with a dead faith, and who declared that a dead faith cannot save a man. 'What doth it profit, my brethren, if a man say he hath faith, but have not works? can that faith save him?'[2]

But our own position is wholly different from that of the people to whom the Christian Gospel was first preached. We have inherited the Christian tradition of thought; we have been trained to Christian habits

[1] Romans x. 9, 10.   [2] James ii. 14.

of life; we were taught the story of Christ in our childhood, just as we were taught the story of our own English kings, and we received each story as a matter of course.

When we come to be in real earnest about finding God and obtaining the forgiveness of sins, and grace to live the Christian life, many of us discover that our belief has done nothing for us. Then we ask whether we are to believe in Christ in some new way, and, if so, in what way. We begin to analyse our faith and to test its worth. We ask whether it is a living faith or a dead faith, and how—if it is a dead faith—it is to be made living. These inquiries obstruct the movement of the soul towards Christ.

While they last a man is wholly occupied with his own thoughts about Christ instead of Christ's thoughts about him. They produce in many cases intellectual confusion and moral discomfort; men grow weary of what seems to be a very profitless employment of time and strength, and very many turn back with a sense partly of disappointment—but partly of relief—to their old life.

Suppose we attempt to approach the subject from another side. Suppose we ask—not what is the condition of receiving forgiveness of sin and the life of God and power to do His will—but what is it to be a Christian? Perhaps by this method we may escape some of the difficulties of which I have been speaking.

II

To be a Christian—that is the great thing. Some men are Christians; some are not; and this is the critical difference between them. Some of us are Christians—really Christians; but, I fear, not all. Two men have the same religious creed: one of them knows that he is a Christian; the other has an uneasy suspicion that he is not. It may sometimes happen, indeed, that a man whose creed is very defective is a Christian, and another whose creed is comparatively full and true is not; it is a loss to a man to have a very defective creed, but if, through God's grace, he is doing the will of Christ up to his knowledge, it is well with him in this world and will be better in the next. Two men may listen to the same sermon and unite in the same prayer; one of them, who has a warm and imaginative temperament, is filled with emotion; the other, whose temperament is colder, is moved very slightly; but the man who is slightly moved may be sure that he is a Christian, and the man who is filled with emotion may have good reason to fear that he is not. Those who are not really Christians may attend worship as regularly as those who are: they may contribute as largely for the relief of the poor and for all kinds of Christian work. What is the difference between these two descriptions of men? If I say that only those are Christians who have a living faith in Christ, I shall give a true answer—and not only a true answer but the answer which reaches to the very root of the difference; but the answer will leave many of you in perplexity. Some of you, knowing that the matter is of very urgent and awful practical importance to yourselves, might ask me to give you a clear account of what is meant by a living faith, and to point out wherein it differs from a dead faith, and this discussion might soon lose all its practical value and have only a metaphysical interest.

Suppose—I repeat—we approach the subject from another side. What is it to be a Christian? To be a Christian is to be a servant of Christ—a slave of Christ. To be a Christian is to belong to Christ, body and soul, as a slave belongs to his master; it is to belong to Christ by our own consent. It is not to serve Christ as a labourer who is hired by the hour, or the day, or the week, but to be in His service always, like a slave in the service of a master who has bought him in the market or has taken him captive in war. No doubt, in the old days of slavery, there was a great difference in the moral worth of slaves: some were faithful and some were unfaithful; some were industrious and did their very best to serve their master; some were indolent and cared very little for their master's interests; but even the most careless knew that he was a slave and thought of himself as a slave: it was his master's work that he had to do and it was his duty to do it well. He might run away, and if he was not caught might so become free; but till then he was a slave and belonged—not to himself—but to another.

And so the Christian man—as long as he is a Christian—is Christ's servant—Christ's slave. He may not be worth much to Christ, and he may know it. He may do his work carelessly, and he may know it. He may be an incapable and inefficient servant, and he may know it. He may steal a large part of his Master's time, and he may know it. He may be careless about his Master's interests, and he may know it. But as long as he is a Christian he knows that his first duty is to do the will of Christ—always and in everything; and that he ought to serve Christ to the utmost of his strength. He is ill at ease if he is not serving Christ earnestly. His conscience is restless. His self-indulgence brings him no real happiness. He, too, may run away—may apostatise—may cease to be a Christian; but till then he is not free—not free except with that deepest and noblest kind of freedom which is found only in the service of our true Lord.

It is observable that when Paul describes himself as the servant of Christ he says that he is the servant of *Jesus* Christ. Jesus is the human name of our Lord; it was the name given to Him at His birth; the name by which His mother called Him when He was living with her as a child at Nazareth; the name by which he was known in His maturer years to his fellow-countrymen. And Peter describes himself in the same way; he is 'a servant and Apostle of Jesus

Christ.'[1] So does Jude; he is 'a servant of Jesus Christ.'[2] So does James; he is 'a servant of God and of the Lord Jesus Christ.'[3] And John in the opening of the Apocalypse speaks of 'the Revelation of Jesus Christ,' which he sent to 'his servant John.'[4]

It is that same Jesus whose gracious words and gracious deeds are recorded in the Four Gospels, whose servants we are to be.

Now, to be the servants of Jesus Christ we must believe and know that Jesus Christ is alive. We cannot in any natural sense of the word be servants of the dead: we may serve the living for the sake of the dead, but the dead themselves we cannot serve. If we are to serve Jesus Christ we must know that He is living, and that He has a real and effective interest in the affairs of this present life and this visible world. For us—if we are His servants—He does not belong to a past generation like the sovereigns, the statesmen, the orators, the great teachers, who in their time exerted an immense influence on the history of the world, but who have passed away, leaving only their memory behind them. He is still living; He belongs to our own age as truly as the statesmen who at this moment are shaping the fortunes of England, Germany, France, America,—as truly as the living poets, philosophers, and scholars, whose writings are enriching the currents of contemporary thought. He is alive, and we are His servants—His slaves. His claims upon

[1] 2 Pet. i. 1. [2] Jude 1. [3] James i. 1. [4] Rev. i. 1.

us come first—take precedence of all others. They are not claims of a speculative kind, but are most real and practical. Your relations to Christ, if you are workmen, are just as real and just as practical as your relations to your employer; your relations to Christ, if you are merchants or manufacturers, are just as real and just as practical as your relations to your bankers, to the people from whom you buy and to whom you sell, to the people to whom you owe money, to the people who owe money to you. You are His servants—His slaves.

It is very easy to miss this obvious truth. The religion of Christ has taken its place among the great religions of the world, and the truths which Christ has revealed concerning God and man have exercised the speculative intellect of genius, have been organised into theological systems and defined in famous creeds. Those who accept that account of God and of the human race and of the relations between God and the human race, which is given in the Christian revelation may very naturally call themselves Christians, just as those who accept the Platonic theory of Ideas may call themselves Platonists, and those who accept the doctrine of predestination, with its logical implications, may call themselves Calvinists, and those who accept Mr. Darwin's theory of development and the origin of species may call themselves Darwinians. But to be really a Christian, something wholly different from the intellectual acceptance of the Christian creed is necessary. Plato, Calvin, Darwin, are all dead men, and I cannot be their servant; and even if they were living men, though I might serve them from affection or from reverence—or they might purchase my service—the service I might render them would be a voluntary service, or the fulfilment of a contract voluntarily entered into; and their authority over me would be very limited. They could not claim me as their property; and if they attempted to put any restraint on my freedom I should resent it. But Christ's authority over me is absolute in this world and the next: I am His servant, His slave.

Again, the religion of Christ contains, not only an account of God and of man and of their mutual relations, but also certain characteristic moral principles for the guidance of life—principles which are intended to inspire and control the conduct of men of every rank and condition. And as a man who accepts the ethics of Epictetus as a practical law of life may call himself a Stoic, so a man who endeavours to regulate his thoughts, temper, words and actions by the ethical principles of the Sermon on the Mount may naturally call himself a Christian. But to be really a Christian something more than the practical acceptance of Christian morality is necessary. I read Epictetus and find in him a great deal to invigorate my moral life and to sharpen the keenness of my moral discernment; but he is my teacher, and only my teacher; I form my own judgment about his precepts; he has no claim on my submission; if I live a good life, Epictetus will give me no reward; if I live a bad life, Epictetus will inflict on me no punishment; my perfection is not to be achieved by recognising in him the supreme authority to which I am accountable for conduct; Epictetus and I are to be judged alike by an august Power that is above us both. But I read the Sermon on the Mount and find myself in the immediate presence of that supreme authority, that august Power; He who speaks is my Lord; I am His servant—His slave; my perfect righteousness is perfect obedience to Him.

This, then, is what is meant by being a Christian. The doctrine of the Person of Christ and of the Atonement of Christ is only an intellectual explanation of the grounds on which the immense claims of Christ to absolute authority over human life rest. Faith in Christ—what theologians call saving faith—is that deep and interior surrender of the soul to Christ which is the root of a glad and exulting consent to acknowledge His authority in conduct. Dismiss for a time all speculations about doctrine, if doctrine perplexes you. Dismiss for a time all restless anxiety about the reality and depth of your faith in Christ. Deal with this question—it is a simple one—and it is intensely practical—Do you, will you, accept the Lord Jesus Christ as your Lord, in the very largest and deepest sense that the words can bear? Do you, will you, consent to be His servant—His slave? The acceptance, the consent carries with it a real faith in Him, and therefore carries with it the forgiveness of sin, the power to maintain a struggle, and a successful struggle, with sin, the peace which comes from the discovery of the love of God, the joy which is inspired by the hope of eternal glory.

Do any of you say that in describing ourselves as the servants, the slaves of Christ, I am forgetting the gracious words of our Lord, in His last discourse? 'Ye are my friends, if ye do the things which I command you. No longer do I call you servants—slaves; for the servant, the slave, knoweth not what his lord doeth: but I have called you friends; for all things that I heard from my Father I have made known unto you.'[1] I have not forgotten those words: who that has read them can ever forget them? But the infinite kindness and condescension of Christ cannot abolish the real relations between Him and me or justify me in disregarding them. If the Queen graciously called me not her subject but her friend, I trust that I should not be guilty of the presumption of forgetting that I was her subject still; and if I did forget I should incur her just rebuke. Nor can I forget that Christ is my Lord and that I am His servant and slave, though He treats me with the confidence of a friend.

On that very evening when our Lord spoke the words which I have quoted, He said to His disciples, 'Ye call Me Master, and Lord: and ye say well; for so I am.'[2] And even when He called them friends,

[1] John xv. 15. [2] John xiii. 13.

the graciousness of His condescension could not conceal His authority: 'Ye are my friends if ye do the things which I command you.'[1] *Which I command you.* He is still our Lord though He makes us His friends. It is impossible for us to call ourselves by any other name than His servants, whatever may be the name by which He calls us. We are infinitely grateful for His goodness in calling us His friends: but for us it is our joy and our glory that He is our Lord; and if He were anything less than that, our blessedness would be destroyed.

Let no one suppose that in this relationship to Christ there is anything hard. May I venture on a personal reference? In a time of great prostration and suffering—the very extremity of mortal weakness—when I sorely needed consolation and support—I recalled the great words in the Epistle to the Hebrews—'He is not ashamed to call them brethren,'[2] and I endeavoured to draw strength from the great and wonderful truth that Christ the Eternal Son of God is our Brother, and clings to us with the tenderness and strength of a Brother's affection; but that truth gave me no comfort; it seemed remote and unreal. Then I remembered that Christ is my Lord, and it steadied me at once, gave me rest of heart and courage and strength. Under other conditions the truth that He calls us His brethren might bring solace and joy; but if I understand accurately how it was with me at that time, the severity and stress of

[1] John xv. 14. [2] Heb. ii. 11.

the suffering and peril demanded something more bracing, something—shall I say—more austere, than the assurance of the brotherly kinship and sympathy of our Lord. It was not sympathy I needed so much as the consciousness of being in the strong hands of One who was my Lord and the Lord of all. It is a truth for times of health and strength as well as of weakness. This, also, is true. We were not created for independence but to be under the absolute authority of Him from whom our life comes and in whom we are to find our blessedness. Till we accept that authority, frankly and joyfully, and stand by our acceptance of it, the regal force which should unite and control and direct all the powers of our nature is absent. One usurping power after another will attempt to rule us; and till the true King is on His throne our life will be like a kingdom which has no settled and well-ordered government. If our nature has strength in it, every vigorous passion in succession will play the tyrant for a time, and draw to itself and its service all our intellectual and emotional energy; if we are weak there will be anarchy; year after year will pass by, and we shall achieve nothing. Christ, and Christ alone, can so rule us as to give us power, freedom, security, wealth, and glory. We are His servants—His slaves. We can never live our true life till we deny and reject all claims to live for ourselves and consent to live for Him.

XIX

THE WORK OF THE MINISTRY

'*Separate Me Barnabas and Saul for the work whereunto I have called them.*'—ACTS xiii. 2.

DURING the last two or three years there has appeared among the Congregational Churches of this country a remarkable deepening of interest in Christian missions to the heathen. There are still, I suppose, large numbers of Congregationalists who regard this great work of God with indifference; and among those of us who have come to care for it there are, perhaps, comparatively few in whom there is what can be properly called missionary enthusiasm. But the fire has been kindled, and it is burning year after year with a brighter and an intenser flame. The men who are most conspicuous for the fervour and energy with which they have urged the claims of foreign missions are happily young men; and they are men who on account of their high character, their religious earnestness, their intellectual distinction, and their eloquence have the largest authority over the thought and action of English Congregationalism. Their power—God's power working through them and in them—has already produced a profound impression. There is a clear prospect of a great and permanent increase in the funds of the London Missionary Society, and it was determined many months ago to strengthen our missionary staff in foreign countries by the addition of one hundred European missionaries.

When that decision was reached I rejoiced in the ardour and hopefulness from which it came; and yet I was uneasy. A hundred men with the qualifications—physical, intellectual, moral, and spiritual—for this work are not to be found easily. I had some fear that the directors of the Society might be under a strong temptation to accept as candidates men of an inferior type, rather than fail to give effect to the wishes of their constituencies. The temptation remains; but I believe that the directors are quite as conscious of the peril as any of us can be; and the policy of immediate extension has been more than justified by the joy, and even the exultation, with which large numbers of Christian men and women have received it. It has greatly intensified, and has spread more widely the renewed interest in missions.

But, as yet, the hundred additional men have not offered themselves—have not been discovered. I have never doubted that if the men were ready to be sent—the right men—the funds necessary to send them out would not be wanting. As it is, the funds will, I hope, soon be ready; but the men—we have to find them.

This raises a question of great importance. It is a question which relates to the work of our churches in this country as well as to their work in heathen and Mohammedan nations. There are large numbers of earnest, thoughtful, able and devout men in the Congregational ministry; there are powerful preachers and wise and gracious pastors; but if there were many more of them we might greatly increase both the number and the usefulness of our churches. We never had a greater opportunity than has come to us now—never a greater opportunity at home, never so great an opportunity abroad. But the men—the fit men—for both departments of work, are too few.

It is true, no doubt, that the effective minister must be qualified for the ministry and called to it by the Holy Spirit; but it does not follow that the Church has nothing to do with his call and his qualifications. When our Lord saw how immense was the work which had to be done, even in His own time and among His own people, He said to His disciples, 'The harvest is plenteous, but the labourers are few: pray ye therefore the Lord of the harvest, that He send forth labourers into His harvest.' The descent of the divine grace and power upon a man to enable him to do work worth the doing in the great harvest-field and the divine impulse which constrains him to do it are—not absolutely, but normally—conditioned by the prayers of the Church. If we do not pray that God will raise up great preachers, great pastors, great leaders of religious thought and life at home, great missionaries to lay the foundations of churches in foreign lands, we are not to expect Him to do it. He *may* do it. An occasional prophet may be sent to us at home without our asking; and apart from our prayers a man here and there may catch the flame of the divine pity for heathen nations; but these will be exceptional manifestations of God's great mercy for ourselves and for all men. He has taken us into fellowship—into partnership—with Himself in saving the world, and the work will move forward sluggishly if we are careless about it.

But it is not only through neglecting to pray to God to give us ministers and missionaries that our churches may fail to obtain them. There may be something—I think there is—in the prevailing thought of modern Congregationalists about the ministry both at home and among the heathen which has the same disastrous effect. We are inheriting the results of all revolts against institutions and authorities which have been long established, and have become corrupt—of all effective protests against false religious conceptions which have for many centuries held ascendency over the human mind. The sacerdotal conception of the Christian ministry,—this we have rejected, and rightly rejected; it is intolerable to us; we trample it under foot. Yes; but the Christian ministry remains; and when a false conception of it is rejected, we have still to find the true, and I am not at all clear that we have taken much trouble to find it. It is a very common error to suppose that if we are passionately hostile against a wrong conception we must be in possession of a right one; but to destroy is comparatively easy, to re-construct is always difficult; and the very passion—the righteous passion—which we feel against the sacerdotal idea of the ministry may prevent us from seeing clearly the spiritual idea of it.

I do not propose, however, to attempt this morning so great and formidable a task as that of illustrating the theory of the Christian ministry as determined by a spiritual conception of the Church. My aim is a much more modest one. I want to discuss some prevailing opinions,—or I might perhaps call them, some prevailing tendencies of thought, among Congregationalists which depreciate the idea of the ministry, and contribute to prevent men from becoming either ministers in England or missionaries to races which are Mohammedan or heathen.

I

And, first of all, there is the earnestness with which many of us have insisted for the last thirty or forty years on the sacredness of industry, commerce, literature, art, and the liberal professions. There has been a vehement protest against any sharp contrast between the religious and the secular life. To the Christian man God is present in the warehouse as well as in the church—there are no sacred places.

God is to be served on Mondays as well as on Sundays—there are no sacred times. The devout blacksmith is as truly a king and priest unto God as his minister—there are no sacred persons.

There were times when, if a young man wanted—to use what was the common phrase—to give his whole life to Christ and to Christ's service, he imagined that the only way by which this could be done was to enter the ministry or to become a missionary. He was impatient till his desire could be satisfied. The months that he was spending at the merchant's desk, or in a solicitor's office, or at a carpenter's bench, seemed lost time; it was not consecrated to Christ. But we have taught our young men, and have taught them rightly, that all Christian men are the servants of Christ, whatever their occupation may be; that He wants men to do carpenters' work and clerks' work and solicitors' work as well as to preach; that Christ is Lord of all the provinces of human life, and that in all of them His servants may faithfully do His will.

Nor is it only in relation to every kind of business and profession that we have asserted this principle. We have also told men that they are to get the will of Christ done in reforming the economic order, in municipal administration, in political movements, in parliamentary contests, in legislation and national policy. We have pointed out the great opportunities which are afforded by all these forms of activity for loyalty to the law and spirit of Christ. We have said, and said very truly, that a member of a Town Council and a member of Parliament may be serving Christ as earnestly as the most faithful pastor in England, or the most fervent missionary in China.

This truth belongs to the very substance of the Christian conception of human life; it is also part of that Gospel which it is the special duty of Protestants to make clear to all men, and to illustrate in their personal life. I thank God that I have seen it actually illustrated in the lives of Christian men whom I have known. But there is no great truth which may not be perverted.

Here is a young man who is aglow with gratitude for the forgiveness of his sins, for access to God through Christ, for power to master temptation and to achieve righteousness; and it seems to him that it would be the blessedness and glory of his life to make known the Christian Gospel in Central Africa, or in China, or in India. He wants to serve Christ with his whole heart and strength, and this seems the way to do it.

But he has a clear prospect of making two or three thousand a year as a solicitor or in a prosperous retail business; or he has a chance of making four or five thousand a year—perhaps eight or ten or even more—as a manufacturer or merchant. He has heard what salaries are received by missionaries; he can imagine to what small economies they are driven if they have children to educate; and he has seen that even these small salaries are criticised and declared to be too large. But he is prepared to make the sacrifice. What sacrifice would he not make while the fires of his love for Christ and for men are rising so high and burning with so pure a flame?

An unnecessary, a wilful sacrifice, however, is what no man is called upon to make; if he does make it, he can hardly hope that God will accept it. If this young man can serve Christ as faithfully in London or Liverpool as in China—as faithfully in a prosperous business or honourable profession as in preaching the Gospel to the heathen—why should he go abroad? Is it not a needless sacrifice?

If he serves Christ—and he may serve Christ—as lawyer, physician, manufacturer, merchant, he may have a pleasant house with gardens round it, a handsome library, and beautiful pictures on his walls; he may shoot in the autumn; he may even keep a yacht; every few years he may be absent from England for several months, and may see Florence, and Rome, and Naples, and Athens, and Constantinople, and Cairo. He may have £2000 or £5000 a year instead of £300. That looks a more attractive life for himself—to say nothing of the wife that he may marry some day, and children that may come to him—than the life of a missionary. If in this delightful manner he can serve Christ—and he can—why should he not do it?

Look at the alternative from another point of view. He knows something of ministers at home. The life of the majority of them probably seems to him rather a cheerless one. Here and there it is different; but no modest man supposes that he will have exceptional success. The earnest, fervent young man whom we are thinking about, looks round and sees that most ministers work hard without achieving, as far as he can see, any remarkable results; they do not count by hundreds the men and women they have rescued from a vicious and sinful life; and the Christian people who have been trained by their ministry are not—all of them—shining saints. Much of the minister's work seems to him rather uninteresting. If he becomes a minister, the chances are that he will be a very ordinary kind of minister, with a small congregation, in a small town, and with a small income. He remembers how he has been moved and stirred by a sermon or a speech about serving Christ in the Town Council or in Parliament. Why should he not remain in business and do that—have a good income—be an alderman—then mayor? It seems to him that there is something stirring and animating in a scheme of life like this. There will be municipal contests to fight, and great schemes for the benefit of the community to be promoted when he is returned. He will be in the inner councils of the local leaders of the political party to which he belongs. He will serve Christ by making speeches that will be received with enthusiastic cheers, and will be praised next morning in the leading articles of local papers. He will help to carry some substantial measure for promoting the health of the community; he will be banqueted for his public services, and his portrait by a famous painter, with an inscription, will be hung up in the municipal buildings. Before his health has given way he will try for the House of Commons; even if he fails, there will be the excitement and glory of the fight; and if he wins, he thinks that all his wishes will be satisfied.

If a man can serve Christ as faithfully in a life of this kind as in the life of a minister—and he can—why should he become a minister?

Before replying to the general question, shall we consider it in relation to a particular case? Soon after Paul crossed from Asia to Europe he met at Corinth Aquila and Priscilla, who were tentmakers. Paul had learned that trade, and he and they worked together. Suppose that the business had prospered, and that after a few months it seemed likely that if they continued to work together they would get a very large trade and an excellent income. Suppose that Paul had then begun to argue that he had been living a very hard life, and that there was no chance of its becoming easier as long as he went about the world preaching the Gospel; that a man could serve Christ just as faithfully in tent-making as in preaching; and that therefore he might as well stay in Corinth, make money, live in a pleasant house, marry, settle down, and spend the rest of his days pleasantly. Would that conclusion have contributed to the honour of Christ, the good of men, or to Paul's own enduring happiness and glory?

Or take another case. John Wesley cared a great deal for the miseries of the poor, and longed to relieve them. He also had a deep conviction that the laws of eternal righteousness should govern the actions of nations as well as of individual men. Suppose that when the evangelistic passion took possession of him he had said, A man may do the will of Christ, and do it faithfully in the House of Commons as well as in the pulpit. Suppose he had been returned for some constituency which would have given him a fair measure of independence in his political action; had joined in the assault on Walpole, and helped to expel him from power; had become, as he was certain to have become, a great member of Parliament; had held office under one minister after another who succeeded Walpole; had been a keen supporter of the war with France; had taken part in settling the terms of peace at Aix-la-Chapelle; had become in his later years a powerful member of the opposition which compelled the King to dismiss Lord Bute; had endeavoured to do what he believed to be the will of Christ by opposing the Stamp Act and all the subsequent policy which led to the declaration of independence by the American colonies; had sacrificed office and sacrificed popularity for many years by his resolute determination to deal with America according to his own convictions of what was just and expedient. Wesley would then have taken a splendid position among the statesmen of his generation, with different, though perhaps equal powers; would have ranked with Chatham, and Fox, and Burke, and Pitt; and his politics would have been as truly controlled by his loyalty to Christ as was his actual work in the foundation of Methodism. But would it have been well for England, for the world, for Wesley himself, for the honour of Christ, that he should have descended from his position as a great preacher to the position of a great member of the House of Commons or a great minister of state? In the case of Paul, in the case of Wesley, how immense would have been the loss to mankind and to themselves if they had served Christ—no matter how faithfully—in any other way than as preachers of the Christian Gospel!

The principle on which the question which we are considering must be determined is simple and obvious. To make tents is a useful and admirable occupation; the tents give protection from rain and cold to the people who use them; enable them to sleep peacefully; may sometimes save their lives. It is the will of Christ that some of His servants should give themselves to tent-making; and if by God's Providence Aquila and Priscilla are destined to the business, they can serve Christ in it as faithfully as Paul can serve Christ in preaching. But preaching is a kind of service incomparably higher than tent-making, demanding natural power and spiritual gifts of a loftier order, achieving results immeasurably more glorious.

That some men should do political work, and give nearly their whole time and strength to it, is one of the necessary results of the order of human life. We are organised into nations, and we must have statesmen to administer our national affairs. Statesmanship affords a Christian man a great opportunity of doing service to Christ and to mankind. And if it is apparent to a man like Wilberforce or Fowell Buxton or John Bright that he is called of God to go into the House of Commons, he may serve Christ just as faithfully as a politician as if he had become the leader of a great religious revival like Wesley. But Wesley's service is of a higher rank; it deals, and deals directly, with interests more awful and more august; its achievements are more enduring and more wonderful.

But it may be said that it is possible for a man to remain in business or to occupy himself with politics, and still to give a considerable amount of time to the highest work of all. At Corinth and at Ephesus, and probably in some other places, Paul worked at his tents and yet preached. Wilberforce was member for Yorkshire, and an active supporter of Mr. Pitt, and yet wrote a religious book, which in its time produced a great impression—*A Practical View of Christian Religion*; and he was one of the leaders of the Evangelical party in its best days.

The two cases are not parallel with each other; nor does either of them touch the point that I want to urge. With Wilberforce, as a member of Parliament, politics were his main occupation; the writing of religious books, the leadership of a religious party, filled up the vacant spaces of a life on which Parliament had the first claim. With Paul, preaching was his main occupation; he worked at tent-making for no other purpose than to earn his bread. He did not set up large works in Corinth or Ephesus; take a long lease of convenient premises; make himself known as the inventor of a new and more convenient kind of tent; enter into engagements that would have prevented him leaving the city at a day's notice. If all the churches that he founded had been like the Church at Philippi, I suppose that he would not have worked at tent-making at all. From the Philippian Christians he was willing to receive help, and he received it more than once; they were kindly and generous people, and had the largest confidence in the apostle's unselfishness. But at Corinth there was a different temper. There were men who watched him suspiciously, and who were eager to be able to say that he was going about preaching with no other object than to get money from his converts; and there were many of the Corinthian Christians whose spirit was so mean that they were quite ready to believe such accusations. Not a penny of theirs would Paul touch. He would be no burden to men who would have felt it burdensome to support him. 'You thought I wanted to rob you—I robbed *other* churches,' he says—'taking wages of them that I might minister to you,' and he had to eke out these contributions from Philippi by working with Aquila and Priscilla at making tents. But, as I have said, his preaching was his first business; everything had to give place to that.

It is true, however, that men who are engaged in trades and professions may do a large amount of work that is, by way of distinction, called religious. They may serve Christ in their business or their profession as faithfully as the minister or the missionary can serve Him—though the service is of a less honourable kind; and they may also serve Christ in the same description of work as that which the minister and the missionary are doing. And I believe that there was never a time in the history of the Christian Church when so large a proportion of Christian men and women gave so large a proportion of their time to religious work as during the last thirty or forty years in England and America.

I should like to see this union of secular and religious work greatly developed. How is it that in the Congregational churches of this country there are so few merchants, manufacturers, lawyers, tradesmen, who are willing to be pastors of the smaller churches, and to do occasional evangelistic work? They have the intellectual vigour that is necessary; they might acquire, if they do not actually possess, the special theological knowledge that is necessary; many of them are effective public speakers. It is not their health that prevents them, or the pressure of their business; for they are members of Town Councils and County Councils; they give a large amount of time to the management of hospitals and to political agitation; they sit on the bench for many hours every week; they are willing to enter Parliament. How is it that they are not pastors and preachers? In past times eminent Welsh ministers —preachers who stirred the hearts of immense congregations and made their power felt through the whole country—had their farms and their trades on which they relied—or relied mainly—for their support; and I believe that there are still a considerable number of ministers in Wales who maintain the wholesome tradition. There is nothing in Congregationalism to prevent a similar custom from arising in England; it would be a solution of some of our most serious practical difficulties.

But I can imagine that if a man in a great business, or with a large practice as a physician or a barrister, discovered that he could not only preach so as to interest and instruct men, but that he had the divine gift—there is no other name for it—which enabled him so to preach the Gospel as to shake the hearts of sinful men and women with fear, and to inspire them with happy and wondering trust in Christ for eternal salvation;—if he discovered that those who were already endeavouring to do the will of Christ learnt from him to attempt a higher form of goodness, and to rejoice in God with a deeper joy, so that sermon after sermon of his had become for ever memorable to them;—if, I say, he discovered this, his passion for this great work would become more intense, and he would be restless and impatient under the business and professional engagements—however honourable they might be in themselves—which limited the time and strength which he could devote to it. Yes, and a divine voice might come to the Church in the very terms which were addressed to the Church at Antioch—'*Separate him for the work to which I have called him.*' How is it that we have not a large number of preachers and pastors who, after accumulating in their business or profession enough to support themselves and their families for the rest of their life, have entered the ministry and consecrated their whole time to the service of the Church and the preaching of the Gospel?

II

But this divine call usually comes to a man in early manhood, before he is finally committed to a business or profession which it is difficult for him to give up. If it comes to any of you, let no prospect of gaining wealth in any other way of life, or of distinction in literature, in art, in science—no hope of doing conspicuous political service to your country—prevent you from obeying it. Listen to no sophistry about the possibility of serving Christ as faithfully in the counting-house, in the studio, in the library of the scholar, in Parliament, as in the Christian ministry.

It is true that the merchant, the scholar, the artist, the politician may do his own work as devoutly as the minister, and may be as unreservedly faithful to God; but the work is of another kind, and is of inferior dignity. And while other men who are called to that lower service may be nobly loyal to Christ, you, if you are called to the ministry, will be faithless to Him unless you become a minister. Others may serve Him as merchants, but not you; as artists, but not you; as scholars, but not you; as politicians, but not you. Your initial act in refusing the work to which He destines you—refusing it because some other way of life promises more ease, more wealth, more reputation, offers keener satisfaction to your tastes or your ambition—taints and poisons the springs of all your action. The awful disobedience may be forgiven—God is merciful; and after sharp chastisement you may be allowed to serve Christ in humble obscurity; but the chances are that the life you have chosen in opposition to the Divine call will be a shameful failure, will bring to yourself no happiness or honour, and will confer no blessing on other men. You will suffer an eternal loss. The remembrance of what you might have been and of what you might have done, will survive your mortal years, and will diminish your joy and your glory in the eternal City of God.

For what a life it is—the life of a man separated by the Holy Ghost from all common pursuits, that he may be a missionary to heathen or Mohammedan races, or a preacher of the Gospel to his own countrymen, and a minister of the Church of Christ! He is in the most intimate partnership with God in the most wonderful and most direct form of the Divine activity for the rescue of the human race from sin and from eternal destruction. It is through him that, for the most part, men discover that they are living in the presence of the Infinite and the Eternal God. The heavens and the earth had not revealed it to them; nor conscience; or if they had had some dim and vague sense of it, the fear and the joy of it had never taken possession of them; but they listen to the preacher, and the glory breaks upon them. It is from him that they learn that the Eternal God is the Lord of conduct, and that in the liberation or restraint of every passion—in every act, according to its motive and intention—in every word and every thought, according to its acknowledgment or rejection of the law of truth, of justice, of kindness, of purity, they are obeying or resisting His Will. Human life, throughout the whole range of its memories and its hopes, its pleasures and its pains, its achievements and its reverses, is seen and felt to be in immediate contact not merely with Eternal Law, but with the will of the Eternal God. This tremendous discovery, I say, usually comes to men through the words of the preacher, and with it a sense of failure and sin which no ethical experience had created. Conscience, in some cases, suddenly exerts terrific power, fastens on a moral habit which the man had suspected to be not wholly defensible, but which he had not allowed himself to condemn; on some act—lying back, perhaps, in remote years—fastens on them with an iron hand, drags the agitated and trembling soul into regions of darkness and terror and fiery torture, where it learns for itself that its fault is not in a single evil habit, or in a single evil action, but in itself—in the very substance and fibre of its life. In this misery and despair the man learns—still from the preacher—that in Christ he has eternal redemption. Perhaps he had known it for years. Perhaps his heart had sometimes been moved by the graciousness of the words and deeds of Christ and by the mystery of His death. But the preacher has been so taught of the Holy Ghost—has had so immediate a vision of things divine—that, while he speaks, it is as if the man actually saw for himself the Son of the Eternal descending from infinite heights of glory, eager, impatient to save the world; and discovers that Jesus Christ, Son of God, Son of Man, is actually at his side to absolve him from sin and to receive him in that very hour into the divine kingdom. This is what comes from Christian preaching in heathen countries and in our own. Is not the life of the preacher wonderful?

Nor is this all. A church is gathered. It assembles week after week to listen to its minister. I say nothing of the worship which it is his distinction to lead; it will be more than enough to speak of his preaching. His people have the story of the Lord

Jesus Christ in their hands; the Sermon on the Mount; His discourse to the twelve during the night on which He was betrayed. They have the Epistles of Paul, and of Peter, and of John. Yes, but the preacher having meditated in solitude on the great revelation of the Divine righteousness and love in Christ, and having invoked the illumination and teaching of the Spirit of God, illustrates some promise of Christ's, and even for those who have clung to it for years it shines with a new glory; it was already a star in the heaven of their thoughts, but for ever afterwards it has the splendour of a sun. Or he speaks of some rebuke addressed by Paul to Christian men at Ephesus or Colosse; and though the people had often read it before, they now for the first time discover its power, and there are some of them whom it humbles, and chastens, and recovers from sins which for years had lessened their religious power and clouded their religious joy. Or it is some precept in the Sermon on the Mount of which he speaks; and while he speaks it is as if a film had been removed from the eye of the soul; the fair ideal of some Christian virtue, which had been only dimly seen before, becomes clear and bright, and from that happy moment there are new endeavours and new achievements in the pursuit of Christian perfection.

Sometimes, in a single sermon, the preacher gives access to a previously unknown province of Christian truth. A devout and earnest man in the congregation has heard of the truth before; the language in which it has been stated has excited his interest and his curiosity; he has tried to learn what the language stood for—to reach the actual fact, the spiritual reality which it represented; but every effort has been hindered. It was as if a huge mountain wall shut him in and prevented him from making any way into the wonderful country which lies beyond. But while he is listening to the preacher, and following what seems perhaps a rugged path of thought, without much interest or much promise in it, he is led into a mountain pass which he had never discovered for himself, and in less than an hour he comes out on the other side, and the unknown land, beautiful and fertile, with meadows and orchards, and wide seas of growing wheat—with flowers of every kind, with shining rivers and noble forests—stretches from his feet to the very horizon. Henceforth, the wealth and the loveliness of it are all his own. In that glorious land he needs the preacher no longer, but it was through the preacher that he found his way into it.

Yes, the preacher does a wonderful work; it is the divine call which alone can authorise a man to attempt it either in Christian or in heathen lands; for divine powers are necessary to do it effectively. But how can we measure the shame and the guilt of the man to whom the call comes and who does not obey it? And how, on the other hand, can we measure the blessedness and the glory of the man who is not disobedient to the heavenly vision, and who, till the solemn moment comes, when his work is done, lives and speaks in the power of the Truth and the Spirit of God?

The divine call is necessary, and special gifts of the Spirit of God are necessary, if a man is to be a true minister or a true missionary. What follows? Is it not one of the supreme duties of the Christian Church, especially in an age like this, to entreat God, in His great love and pity for mankind, to separate men from their very birth to this great service; to endow them with the natural force which is necessary for it; to subject them during childhood and youth to the discipline at once gracious and stern which will give them the strength and the gentleness and the knowledge of the heart of man which are required by the preacher; to fill them with the light and power of the Holy Spirit for ministering to others when they have made the Christian redemption their own; and then to call them to the ministry by a voice so pathetic, so sovereign, so awful, that it shall be impossible for them to resist it? God alone can call men to the ministry and qualify them for it. Is there nothing, then, for us to do but to wait until He calls and qualifies? That is not Christ's teaching. '*Pray ye*, therefore, the Lord of the harvest, that He send forth labourers into His harvest;' and let the general opinion and judgment of the Church attribute so lofty a dignity and so sacred a glory to the Christian ministry, that when the prayer is answered and the divine call comes to a man, he shall receive it with trembling joy; and however brilliant may be the promise of any other life that is possible to him, shall exult in the grace which has called him to the honour and blessedness of making known to mankind the infinite love and the awful righteousness of God and the power of the Christian redemption.

XX[1]

'It is high time to awake out of sleep: for now is salvation nearer to us than when we first believed.'—ROMANS xiii. 11.

THE Jews alone, of all ancient races, found their golden age in the future—not in the past. It is remarkable that the tradition of the fair garden of the Lord seems never to have kindled their imagination, or to have awakened their regret. Psalmists and prophets never look back upon the lost joys of Paradise; they always look forward to the transcendent glories of the kingdom of the Messiah.

And the golden age of the Church lies, not in the past, but in the future. We may be humiliated by the passionate devotion to Christ which glowed in the hearts of the apostles and of many of their immediate converts; we may wonder at the courage and fortitude which during the early Christian generations confronted fearlessly all that was mightiest and most venerable in the ancient civilisation, and endured imprisonment, torture, and death in the power of an exulting hope and a triumphant faith; but it is apparent, both from the apostolic epistles and from later Christian writings,

[1] Preached on the first Sunday of the New Year, 1895.

than even in those heroic times there were vast numbers of Christian men and women who fell far short of the saintly life. The glory of God which dwells in the Church of every age was clouded then, as it is clouded now, by human infirmity and sin.

Nor do we look back with regret upon the brief years during which our Lord Himself was visibly present in the world: it was expedient for us that He should go away. The great hour is yet to come: we move forwards to it day by day, year by year. '*Now is salvation nearer to us than when we first believed.*'

The apostle Paul—at least during the early years of his apostolic life—expected that in his own time, before he died, the Lord Jesus Christ would visibly appear in the glory of the Father with His angels; that suddenly the heavens would be all aflame with splendour; that Christ would be seen sitting on the throne; that the dead in Christ would rise; that then those who were alive and longing for His appearing would pass through a most wonderful change; and that then, with songs of thanksgiving and gladness and triumph, and amid the acclamation of the shining hosts of angels, all the children of God would pass to their eternal home. In his Epistle to the Philippians, on the other hand, when writing of the coming of Christ he speaks of departing to be with Christ, which for himself would be far better than remaining in the flesh.[1]

It may be—who can tell?—that there is no real

[1] Phil. i. 23.

inconsistency between these two conceptions of the future. When the hour of Paul's martyrdom came, he may have seen that Christ had actually come in His great glory: when his eyes closed upon the cruel crowd of the heathen who were triumphing in his death, they may have opened at once upon all the majesty and terror of the vision for which he had been hoping. To him, the moment of his own departing to be with Christ may have been the moment of Christ's glorious coming which he had been long expecting; and to every Christian man that has died since, the hour of death may have brought the same experience. To the people in the far east the sun rose this morning ten or twelve hours ago; while the sky was still dark with us, and we had hours of sleep before us, they saw the dawn and said, 'He is risen.' Our time came three or four hours ago; then we saw the dawn and said, 'He is risen.' There are people farther west to whom the heavens are still dark: the dawn is but just breaking on the inhabitants of Boston and New York; they are but just beginning to say, 'He is risen.' And it may be that in the revolution of the ages, every generation as it passes into the world unseen discovers that the splendours of Christ's second coming are just breaking upon it—and they gaze upon Him with joy or with terror. Generation after generation as it sees the invisible world may exclaim, 'He has come.' That great day of the Lord may be a long day extending through many centuries. The dead in Christ rise first; they rise, one generation after another, as His voice reaches them : only when at last the evening comes will those who are still alive be changed, and the history of the world be brought to a close.

I repeat, the sun does not rise every morning at the same moment to the human race of all lands : he rises at successive moments to the people living in different degrees of longitude ; when he rises the day for them begins. And the *Parousia*—the manifestation of the glory of Christ—may not come at the same moment to the human race of all centuries ; it may come at successive moments to the people of successive generations.

But however this may be, our salvation—our final and complete salvation—lies still in the future. We have to die and to rise from the dead—or we have to pass through a great change,—before we reach our eternal perfection and our eternal blessedness.

With that curious delight in half-truths which characterises so many minds, there are people who rebuke us when we talk of a future salvation. They tell us with a great air of originality—as though they had discovered something which had never been thought of before, or had been forgotten for hundreds of years—that Christ brings men a present salvation : that instead of thinking and talking about some wonderful deliverance in the future we ought to think and talk of a wonderful deliverance that Christ will achieve for us now ; that we must live an upright and Christian life now, if we are to inherit eternal glory.

Well—but there is nothing startlingly original in that. Christ saves us now,—that is true: but one of the powers by which He saves us is the hope of a complete salvation hereafter; and if we forget the future salvation, our present salvation will be less complete than it might be.

But death, they say, can work no moral or spiritual change in a man. What a man is on this side of death he will be on the other. There will be no sudden elevation of temper and spirit as the result of passing into another world; the man himself in his real inner life will remain the same.

Yes: I too believe that the man in his real inner life will remain the same. If there is revolt against God's authority, distrust of God's love, ingratitude for God's goodness here—selfishness, wilfulness, impurity here—the revolt, the distrust, the ingratitude, the selfishness, the wilfulness, the impurity will not be cleansed away from a man by the cold waters of the dark river which separates this life from the life to come.

But suppose that there is love for God, though it is wanting in fervour; trust in God, though it sometimes vacillates; gratitude to God, though it is less deep and intense than it should be: suppose—with whatever occasional failures a man is trying to fight the good fight against the powers of darkness,—that he hates the sin which sometimes overcomes him and delights in the righteousness which he too often fails to achieve—will there be no change for him when he passes into the immediate presence of God?

Here is a plant which finds it hard to live under the frosts and mists of these northern skies; it wants warmth; it wants the glowing light of southern lands. See how poor and thin its leaves are; how faint and dull its colour. The plant itself and all the shoots which come from it can reach no perfection. Take it south: the inner life of the plant will not be changed: hemlock will not be changed into a rose; but if it is a *rose*, how it will rejoice in the change! what fulness will come to its leaves, what brilliance to its blossom. If the original plant, having suffered much from an ungenial climate, never reaches consummate beauty, see what will come, in time, from the shoots which are taken from it. And for myself I hope that when we are completely delivered—as we are already delivered in part—from this present evil world; when, instead of having our home in an earthly city with its sins, its miseries, its ambitions, impurities, falsehoods, and strife, we are walking the golden streets of the City of God; when we shall live with saints; when we shall see the face of God as we cannot see it now; and when we shall be completely one with Christ;—I hope that then the life which we have received from God—and which we shall continue to receive from Him—will manifest itself with a power, a grace, a glory, which in this world it cannot achieve.

Paul appeals to the fact that this salvation is nearer to us now than when we first believed,—to induce Christian men to '*awake out of sleep*,' to shake off their indifference to the great duties and the great glories of life.

It was true, of course, of those who had passed from heathenism or Judaism into the Church only a few months before the Epistle was written, that when Paul wrote their salvation was nearer than when they first believed. And it is true this morning that salvation is nearer to the youngest of you than it was when you came into the Church last year or the year before. But it is clear that Paul was thinking of those who had been believers in Christ for ten or fifteen years or more. It is when some considerable time has passed by after the beginning of the Christian life that the appeal in the text becomes most urgent and most effective. And it is to those who are in middle life or who have passed beyond middle life, that I want to speak especially before I close.

As long as I can remember, the chief solicitude of the Church has been concentrated on young people, and it has been for the young that most of its special and exceptional efforts have been made. There are excellent reasons for this which I need not state. But I have often felt and have sometimes said that we have not been anxious enough and have not done enough for those who have long passed the years of their youth. The religious perils of men and women who are over forty are probably greater than the religious perils of those who are under twenty-five; and these perils are increased because the Church does not show a more vivid sense of their gravity. It is not in the cool of the early morning, but when the sun has risen with fervent heat, that the seed sown in rocky places is withered up and perishes. It is not in the early spring, but when the summer has come and the wheat has shot high above the ground, that it is choked by the thorns which have grown up with it so that it bears no fruit. And it is when a man has been in the Church for ten, twenty, or thirty years, that he is in danger of losing the animation and the vigour of his religious life and of sinking into that sleep from which in the text he is called to awake.

With growing years a man's thoughts and heart are in danger of being filled more and more completely with the interests of this passing existence. The young man has not enough in his life to fill all its unoccupied spaces and to task all his strength. He has vague and indefinite cravings which wait for their satisfaction. He stands alone; no heavy responsibilities fill him with anxiety. As the years go on he marries, and he has to care for his wife and his children. Interests of many kinds multiply, until at last, unless faith in God and the vision of eternal things have secured a firm ascendency over him, and are strong enough to resist the increasing pressure of the common affairs of life, they will cease to have any power over him at all. It is the same with women. When they are girls there are open spaces enough in life for imagination, fancy, dreams of their future: when Christ comes with His authority and His love, there is room for Him: He is welcomed; His presence adds immeasurably to their strength and joy. But afterwards the mind and heart get filled. There is the love of husband and children: there is the happiness of a pleasant home; or, if the home is troubled, there are its vexations and anxieties; there is the care of a large household, or the incessant thought and toil which are necessary in the houses of the poor. If men and women live a solitary and unmarried life there are growing difficulties of other kinds.

And so when middle age comes, though there may still be religious life, it is too often asleep. It is inactive—restless perhaps, at times half awake, roused now and then—but not really awake, laborious, energetic. It is asleep, and is not conscious, as it once was, of all the great things by which it is surrounded in that eternal world to which it really belongs.

Some of you know how all this has come about. In youth there was a certain natural ardour which was kindled by prayer and by religious thought: there was a glow and animation in religious worship. You took fire when you sang hymns of passionate thanksgiving to Christ, or when you heard a sermon that had vigour and vehemence in it. With the cooling of your natural temperature, this pleasant excitement has greatly sunk, and the whole realm of religious life has become grey, cold, and comparatively uninteresting.

You hoped, when you began to live for Christ, that you would soon become a saint, and you were disappointed. You did not understand that, though by the growth of the power of Christian faith, you would master one set of temptations after another, the conflict would never come to an end; that as you came nearer to Christ, you would discern more and more of your unlikeness to Him; that although you ought to discover proofs that you were really serving Him, in the increasing obedience that you were rendering to His commandments, you were never to find any satisfaction and self-complacency in your own sanctity, but were to find an ever-deepening joy in His perfection and in His grace. And this, perhaps, disheartened you. You became weary of pursuing a perfection which retreated from you as the horizon retreats, the more rapidly, the more rapidly you were approaching it. You became weary of fighting new temptations, after you had conquered old temptations. You gradually began to compromise with the world and the flesh, and, though you did not know it, with the devil too.

And now, at the very time when your religious life ought to be most vigorous, you are conscious of its weakness. Now is the time, when by the energy of your faith, you ought to have been the strong support of those whose faith is faltering. Now is the time when your love for God, though the flame of early years had sunk, should be burning at a white heat, and adding to the fervour of the love of all your Christian brethren. Now is the time when, as the result of prolonged Christian experience, your power for Christian work should have been at its best. Now is the time when your intercessions for others ought to have become most effective. Now is the time when your Christian men should have been able to look to you, and to see how possible it is for Christian men to be living in God—to breathe the atmosphere of heaven—even while the cares of this world are pressing upon them most heavily. But you are conscious that it is not so.

Is it not time '*to awake out of sleep*'? I have noticed, upon a long voyage, that when the ship has been out a week or two, many of the passengers grow listless, and seem to feel the monotony of their life; but as she comes near the port they wake up, become animated, think and speak of their preparations for landing, and of the new interest of their life on shore.

And we are nearer port this morning than when we first believed—how near we cannot tell. '*It is time to awake out of sleep. Now is salvation nearer to us than when we first believed*'—ten, twenty, thirty, forty, fifty years nearer: within a few months, within a few weeks, the glory of it may be manifested. Let our minds dwell on the wonder and blessedness of it. We shall pass—very soon perhaps—into the eternal light. We shall see the very face of Christ. We shall grasp the hands of the saints of other generations. We shall begin to live the new and noble life of the sons of God, who are at home with their Father in heaven. We shall escape from all our infirmities and all our sins. We shall no longer be in peril of missing our eternal inheritance, but shall be safe—safe for ever—within the walls of the City of God. There will be an indefinite expansion of every power and capacity for knowledge and for joy. Every devout affection will become more fervent. We shall begin to serve God with an energy which will never be weary, and with a zeal which will never grow cold. Think of that life—how great it is, how blessed—and surely you will awake out of sleep. Your wealth, your poverty—what are they all in the presence of that wonderful life which is coming so near? Your successes, your disappointments, your schemes for the future, your cares about the present, your pleasures and your vexations, all the pursuits in which you are so keen,—what are they compared with that larger, higher life? There is something to thrill you in the contrast between the life which will soon be over, and the life which will soon begin—something to startle you out of sleep.

That great life—if you but think of it and remember that it is so much nearer to you than when you first believed—will kindle in you a passion of gratitude to God that will make sleep impossible. What infinite grace God is revealing to you in giving you a life like this—and what transcendent power! He will soon lift you—*you*—from all the confusions and agitations which surround you now, into His eternal peace. Your sins, which merited a far different destiny, will be all forgotten. You have often distrusted the goodness of your Heavenly Father, have been impatient of His discipline, have done the things which He has commanded us not to do, left undone the things which He has commanded us to do—cared too little for His approval, too much for the approval of man—and even for the approval of men who had no love for Him; but you are His children, and you are to know the honour and the joy of sonship. Ah! what a life it will be. The beginning of it is nearer than when we first believed: but look on beyond its beginning, to age after age of righteousness unstained, peace untroubled, joy unclouded, knowledge ever widening, fellowship with God and with the saints becoming ever more intimate, glory passing into diviner glory, through countless millenniums of blessedness. Gratitude for this eternal and perfect life should so stir your heart as to make sleep impossible.

The '*salvation is nearer than when we first believed.*' Whatever effort—painful effort it may be—we have to make; whatever sacrifices we have to endure—if we awake and begin to live that vigorous Christian life, which has been too long delayed—will be soon at an end, and the glory will come. The time is short during which we can do the will of God, on earth, with all our heart—can serve Him with happy love and resolute fidelity, and serve men for His sake. Let none of it be wasted. From this hour let it be apparent that we are at last awake—and that with new and larger conceptions of the claims of God upon all that we are and all that we have, we are resolved to live the perfect life.

www.ingramcontent.com/pod-product-compliance
Lightning Source LLC
LaVergne TN
LVHW020531100826
845148LV00010B/1426

* 9 7 8 1 5 9 7 5 2 6 4 4 9 *